Time
Management

Polly Bird

TEACH YOURSELF BOOKS

DEDICATION

1703 7194 15

To the person who invented the wastepaper bin.

For UK order queries: please contact Bookpoint Ltd, 39 Milton Park, Abingdon, Oxon OX14 4TD. Telephone: (44) 01235 400414, Fax: (44) 01235 400454. Lines are open from 9.00 - 6.00, Monday to Saturday, with a 24 hour message answering service. Email address: orders@bookpoint.co.uk

For U.S.A. & Canada order queries: please contact NTC/Contemporary Publishing, 4255 West Touhy Avenue, Lincolnwood, Illinois 60646-1975, U.S.A.. Telephone: (847) 679 5500, Fax: (847) 679 2494.

Long renowned as the authoritative source for self-guided learning – with more than 30 million copies sold worldwide – the *Teach Yourself* series includes over 200 titles in the fields of languages, crafts, hobbies, sports, and other leisure activities.

Library of Congress Catalog Card Number: On file

First published in UK 1998 by Hodder Headline Plc, 338 Euston Road, London, NW1 3BH.

First published in US 1998 by NTC/Contemporary Publishing, 4255 West Touhy Avenue, Lincolnwood (Chicago), Illinois 60646 – 1975 U.S.A.

The 'Teach Yourself' name and logo are registered trade marks of Hodder & Stoughton Ltd.

Typeset by Transet Limited, Coventry, England.
Printed in Great Britain for Hodder & Stoughton Educational, a division of Hodder Headline Plc, 338 Euston Road, London NW1 3BH by Cox & Wyman Ltd, Reading, Berkshire.

Impression number	10	9	8	7	6	5	4	3	2
Year			2002	2001	2000	1999	1998		

TEACH YOURSELF BOOKS

Time
Management

CONTENTS

ACKNOWLEDGEMENTS

Thank you to Joanne Osborn at Hodder & Stoughton and Teresa Chris, my agent. I also thank my husband, Jon, whose forbearance and support are, as always, invaluable.

Polly Bird. Chester, 1997

INTRODUCTION

This book is a jargon-free guide to the basics of time management – the art of organising your life so that you are in control. You do not need complicated equipment, a staff of dozens, or a six-month break to learn how to save time and achieve more. All you need is a willingness to try some of the ideas in this book and the energy to start now.

Time management is easy. All you have to do is rearrange the way you work and use the time you save effectively. That's all there is to it.

Most of us muddle through our lives fitting in things where we can. We have a few things that demand fixed attendance from us, such as work, college or prearranged leisure pursuits. But the rest of the time we make do and hope that everything will fall into place.

The feeling we are left with is one of frustration. There never seems to be enough time for everything that we need or want to do. This leads to stress and chaos in our lives. Our work and home life suffer and we see time slipping away from us.

Time management is the answer to this. It will help you control time by deciding what you do with it and when you want to do it. Far from being a rigid way of living, it frees you to get on with the important things in your life.

The benefits of managing your time include an increase in productivity as you take control of what you do and when you do it. You also get more time for rest and recreation – the important recharging of your batteries that helps you cope with what life throws at you.

Time management involves recording, monitoring and improving how you use your time. Once you know how your time is usually spent, you can make sensible decisions about how to use it better.

But however well you plan your time you will not make the best use of it if you indulge in time-wasting activities. By eliminating unnecessary or inefficient tasks, you free up more time for your priorities whether at work, home or leisure.

This book starts by asking you what you want to do with your life and explains how to work out how you really spend your time. It helps you to find out what you do that wastes time and tells you how to eliminate it. Next, it shows you how to plan your time better so that you deal with important activities and tasks at the most appropriate times. It tackles time-wasting activities such as paperwork, phone calls and meetings. And just to make sure that you are not the only person in your office who is working at optimum efficiency, it explains how to instil good time management practices into your staff.

You don't need to spend months on learning the techniques here. You can learn them quickly by reading this book. Put them into practice one at a time and gradually work up to a more effective and less stressful life at work and at home.

Don't panic if you lapse. Just start again and after a while your new way of organising your life will become a habit.

By the time you have finished this book, you will not only be using your time more effectively but will have more of it. This book will help you turn time into your best friend rather than your worst enemy.

1

CHOOSE YOUR PERSONAL PRIORITIES

This chapter encourages you to visualise your future. It tells you how to decide what your priorities and your goals in life are. It explains how to work out what goals to set yourself and the objectives for achieving those goals. By the end of the chapter you will have a clear idea of where you are going and what you want to achieve.

Where are you going?

Like most people you probably take a short-term view of your life. You want to get your work done and get home and have enough time to enjoy yourself. But unless you take a longer view and know where you want your life to go, you cannot plan how you will get there.

You probably live your life in a rush. You rush to get to work, the work piles up, you always seem to be dashing about and never seem to have time to do everything. You probably have times when you feel overwhelmed by the amount you have to fit into your day. You find yourself reacting to other people's demands, interruptions and phone calls instead of controlling your life. This can make you feel stressed, tired and depressed.

But look at the successful people you know. How do they fit so much into their lives but still remain on top of things? The saying 'If you want something done, ask a busy person' fits them well. Yet they never seem overwhelmed by everything. They can fit so much in because they have a clear idea of what they want and where they are going in life. They also have a clear idea about how they are going to achieve it.

By having this clear vision of the future they become successful, busy and happy because they are controlling their time in order to achieve their aims in life. Just as a company with no overall vision founders in the market place, so you will founder in your life unless you know where you are going.

—— Are you Bob or Betty? ——

Be honest with yourself – which of these two people do you resemble most?

Bob regularly oversleeps, gets to work late and feels constantly tired. His desk is covered with piles of paper and he can never find the piece he needs. Work seems never-ending. He constantly has to deal with interruptions either in person or by phone. He dashes from one meeting to another and never seems to have time to settle down to work on his major project. There seems to be a crisis every day. He usually works late, gets home tired and after a hurried meal does more work. His family complain that they hardly see him. He feels frustrated because he never seems to get work done and is constantly under stress. His managers are beginning to wonder if he's really up to the job.

Or are you like Betty? Betty gets up at the same time every morning and allows herself time to have a good breakfast before getting to work on time. She has just as much work to do as Bob but manages to keep it under control. Her desk is not exceptionally neat but has fewer bits of paper on it and is reasonably tidy. She has organised her office so that she can find everything she needs quickly. She too gets interrupted but not nearly as often as Bob and she deals with most interruptions quickly. She only goes to the meetings she needs to and makes sure she is well prepared for them. She has been working on her major project regularly for the past fortnight and it is nearly finished. Fewer crises come Betty's way than Bob's, and those that do she copes with without fuss. She rarely works late and only takes work home occasionally – and then works for an hour at most. She has plenty of time to relax with her family and has the energy to enjoy outside interests. Her managers see a competent employee who has work under control and a personality enriched by her leisure activities. She is earmarked for promotion.

Most of us want to be like Betty but spend more time in a muddle like Bob. But there is hope for you. This book is going to make you efficient and effective.

The 80/20 principle

Did you know that only 20 per cent of your time produces 80 per cent of your work, or that 20 per cent of your work achieves 80 per cent of results, or that 20 per cent of managers do 80 per cent of the work, or ... Examples of this principle are found everywhere. It is also called Pareto's Law after the Mr Pareto who discovered this interesting ratio.

What this means to you is that just 20 per cent of your time deals with productive activities. The other 80 per cent is lower priority or unnecessary.

This shows the importance of working out exactly what you want from life. Once you have defined your goals you must make achieving them the highest priority and use that important 20 per cent of your time and effort on them. That way you will achieve more with less effort.

Your goals will help you prioritise. If something helps you achieve your goals, is an objective or step on the way to one of those goals, then it is high priority. Those important steps will make up the 20 per cent of your work. Put most of your effort into them. The other 80 per cent can be done later, delegated or ignored.

Start taking control

You need a clear idea about how you see your life in the future. Instead of responding to life by giving in to the demands of others, reacting to crises, or simply doing things out of habit, you can control your life. But to do so you need to know what you really want.

What do you want to be doing in five years, ten years, twenty years? What do you want to have achieved by the time you retire? How do you want to spend your retirement? Aim to make your life as much like your dreams as possible. Defining your goals and objectives in life will help you achieve your dreams – or at least go a long way towards them.

By defining your goals you can organise your life accordingly. At first it might seem as if you can't fit everything in. But trust me – if you know clearly where you want to get to, the journey will be much easier.

——— Define your life's key areas ———

First, decide which are the most important areas of your life – your key areas. Look at the various roles you play. Are you a worker, parent, churchgoer, committee member, sports person? By looking at these roles you can work out what broad categories your life falls into. Ask yourself 'What is important to me?' A typical list might be:

- family
- work
- leisure
- community
- religion
- money
- health.

Within each of these areas of your life you will have goals you want to achieve. Until you have worked out what those goals are, you cannot decide what you need to do to achieve them and therefore how to arrange your time to achieve them.

What are your secret ambitions?

Forget for a moment about the work you have to do tomorrow and that committee meeting you have to go to at the local community centre. Take an hour to write down your hopes and dreams – all the things that you want to do, however silly they seem. Include dreams and ambitions that relate to the all the key areas of your life, both professional and private. For example:

- become chief executive
- work only four hours a day
- spend three months fishing in Scotland
- live in China
- go bareback riding in the USA
- buy a Rolls Royce.

Don't be shy – let your dreams flow. Some of the dreams may be ultimately unachievable (perhaps becoming chief executive is a little ambitious!) but they give you something to aim for. Other things, such as the fishing in the example, can be planned for and could be achieved, if you had time and money.

Take into account the things you regret not having done, your secret wishes, the things you like doing best, what you would do if you had more free time, in fact anything that you can visualise as part of your ideal life.

Don't write down what you or other people think you ought to want to achieve – write down your own goals however silly they may seem. If you aim for the stars you might never get there but you can at least visit a few asteroids on the way.

Try to write at least one goal, preferably three, for each key area. For example, suppose your goals for family life are:

- spend more time with my family
- travel together
- have time to help my children with their homework
- spend quality time with my partner.

By writing down your ambitions in this way you can see in which areas you need to make changes to your time.

What talents do you have?

Write down all your talents and inner strengths, too. These are all part of the resources that will help you reach your goals. Don't underestimate these. No skill or personal resource is too trivial to be valuable to you whether it is courage, needlework, honesty, car mechanics, being a good listener or having the ability to get on well with others. Assess all your talents and skills to see how they can help you achieve your goals, or whether they should become part of your goals.

TIME MANAGEMENT TIP

If you are not sure what personal qualities you have, ask a friend to give you an honest assessment.

Define your values

Your goals will give your life direction. However, you also need to think about what your values in life are because these will give meaning to your goals. Ask yourself 'What values are important to me?' It could be anything – family, God, honesty, hard work, compassion. The list will reflect your personal values.

You need not tell anybody what your values are but they will affect whatever choices you make and whether your goals have value for you. You will ask of your goals 'Do they contribute to my values? If not, are they worth pursuing? Or can I change my goals to reflect my values?'

When making a choice about a task, you can ask 'Does this task reflect the importance of my values? Does it contribute to the way I want to live my life?' In effect you are asking yourself 'Do I really want to do this?' of every project and activity you undertake. Of course, there will be things that you have to do as part of your work and private life. But you can do them according to your values and prioritise them according to your goals.

Objectives or major tasks

Now that you have your goals sorted out, write down what you need to define the objectives that will help you to reach them. Record everything you need to do to achieve them. For example, in your key area of work, the objectives you need to achieve to become chief executive might be:

1 Get promotion every three years for the next nine years.
2 Impress the board with my financial acumen.
3 Get known around the company. (See Figure 1.)

Be realistic

Both objectives and steps need to be realistic and achievable. You may never achieve some of your goals entirely but many of the objectives in your key areas can be achieved. Unless you make them realistic you will be constantly frustrated by not achieving them and will probably give up trying. So your objectives need to be:

- attainable – a realistic objective
- specific – so you know exactly what you need to do
- measurable – so you know when you have achieved them
- worthwhile – they contribute to goals and objectives you deem important
- positive – so that you feel good when you have achieved them
- capable of being changed or developed – in case you change your goals.

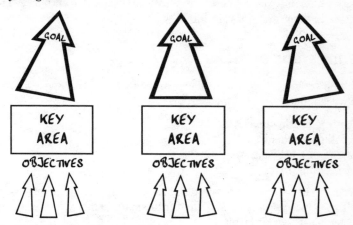

Figure 1   Key areas, goals and objectives

For example, suppose you want to spend time travelling with your family (a goal of a key area in your life – your family) but are limited to three weeks' holiday a year. Perhaps you could investigate weekends away. The same could apply to spending quality time with your partner. Perhaps you both seem to be so busy that you never have any quiet time just to be together and talk. In that case, you would need to look at how you spend your time and see whether everything you do is necessary or important to you. (I deal with how to get out of unnecessary commitments in later chapters.) Or perhaps you could combine travel and quality time by spending weekends away with your partner while a relative baby-sits?

If your goal is general, for example spending more time with your family, you need to find a specific objective to help you achieve your goal. It needs to fit the criteria above and be worthwhile, measurable, positive and changeable.

The specific objective is thus to spend a weekend away with your partner. It is attainable because you can work out how to do it. It is worthwhile and measurable – if you haven't been away you haven't achieved it. It is positive because it will make you (both) feel good and can be changed or developed – you could go somewhere else for another weekend or spend a week away.

By choosing realistic objectives that are measurable and have a positive outcome, you reinforce the achievement and are encouraged to achieve in other areas of your life.

Minor steps or tasks

Each objective can be broken down into smaller steps. For example, the weekend away would involve:

- getting holiday brochures
- booking weekend
- arranging baby-sitter
- arranging travel.

These smaller steps can be slotted into your days. By breaking down each goal into objectives, and then into small, achievable steps, you can achieve them bit by bit.

Prioritising your goals and objectives

Once you have decided what your ambitions are (your goals), however surprising, and have worked out what you need to do to achieve them (your objectives), you need to prioritise them.

This is important because you want to make sure that, when you decide to do something, it contributes to one of your goals or objectives. Some of these priorities are more important than others, so number your lists in order of importance.

Everything you do from now on should contribute in some way to one of your goals or objectives. If it doesn't, why are you doing it?

When making choices ask yourself 'Will it help me reach my goal in this area of my life?' At work the goals will be specific and you should get into the habit of asking yourself 'Will doing this help me achieve this objective?' By doing this you will do the things that most contribute to your goals and the other things will be delegated or done later, or even not at all. So you are already starting to utilise your time more productively.

Yearly, monthly and weekly goals

The goals you have chosen are what you want to do with your life and the objectives you are aiming at will help you achieve those goals. Now think about your goals in shorter time spans. What do you want to achieve by the end of the year? By the end of the month?

Write down your aims and prioritise them. Then break down each aim into smaller steps and prioritise these also. This way you can see everything that you need to fit into the coming time.

Once you have got that sorted out do the same for your weekly goals. Divide each goal into the steps you need to take to achieve it and prioritise them.

So, a goal in your key area of work might be to become chief executive. An objective that contributes to this might be to get promotion within two years. The steps that help you reach your objective might be: to pass the qualifying exams; to impress the interview board; to impress your bosses. Even smaller tasks that contribute might be: go to revision classes; study past papers; learn exam techniques; take classes in interview techniques; read company reports and newsletters; complete a major project on time; present new proposal; help with Christmas concert. (See Figure 2.)

Write your goals at the front of your diary or planner (more about choosing and using these in Chapter 3) so that you always have them in front of you. Look at them every day and reassess them every year. Your values and goals might change. If so, you need to take account of these changes when working out your objectives and tasks.

What you are doing is working out a strategic plan. You are devising plans to help you reach your goals and working out stratagems for achieving those goals. That is the way successful people work.

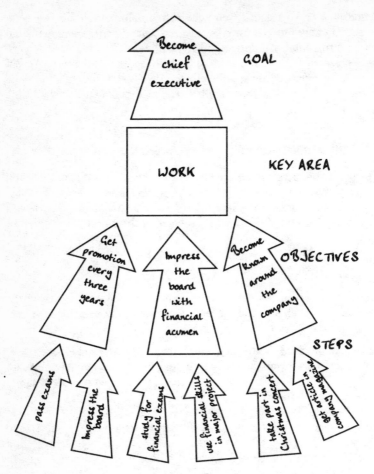

Figure 2   Steps and objectives to reach a goal

Spider diagrams

Setting goals and objectives seems fine, but suppose having tried it your mind goes blank? Suppose you can't work out what your goals in life are? You might never have consciously thought more than a short time ahead and have just lived life as it comes.

If you found it hard to do there is a way of freeing your thoughts. It is called a spider diagram and is useful not only for finding your goals but for finding ideas on all sorts of occasions.

Many people find it hard to talk about themselves to strangers because they are not used to revealing so much of themselves in public. Trying to put thoughts on paper is like making them public. It is particularly hard when you are trying to think in the linear way of lists that we are so used to. A spider diagram releases you to think more in the way we naturally do, that is, jumping from one subject to another.

Take a blank sheet of paper, write your name in the middle and draw a circle round it. Around this write the key areas of your life that you want to think about, for example, work, family, leisure, community life, religion, and so on. Draw circles round these and join them to the centre circle. Take each outer circle in turn and write down anything that comes into your mind about the subject. Write these thoughts down and join them with a line to the relevant circle – either the original or another. Add other ideas by lines to any of the original circles. Don't think 'goals', just think of anything that comes to mind. As you do this you will get a mass of circles and lines connecting each other. (See Figure 3.)

Themes will emerge – perhaps you will discover that particular aspects of work are more important to you than others.

If the chart gets crowded, take one of the circles, for example finances, and put it in the centre of another sheet and continue. (See Figure 4.)

When you have done as much as you can, look at your diagrams and see where you are concentrating your efforts. It will jog you into thinking about your life and what you really want out of it. It will not define your goals as such, but will free your thoughts.

If you want to focus it more, put one subject in the centre, for example work, and then surround it by all the people connected with work, or all the sections of your work, or start from one person, for example, the boss, and think of all the areas of work that you need to improve on to please them.

A spider diagram will help you sort out the essential parts of your life. You can then focus on each part to see what aims you have for it.

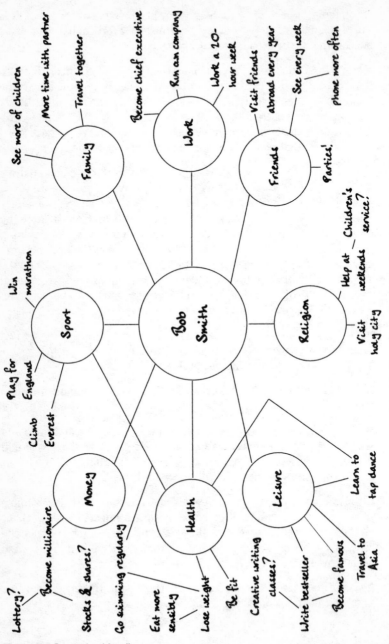

Figure 3 General spider diagram

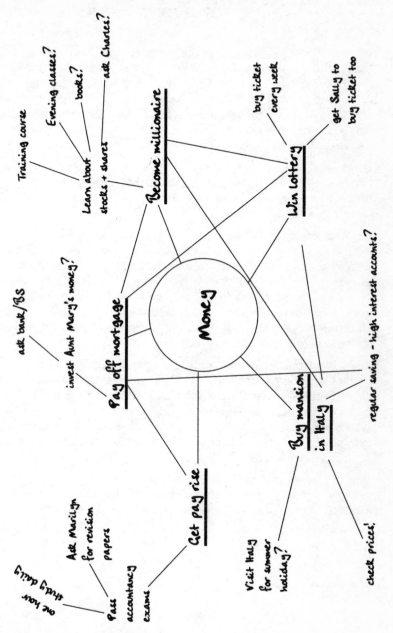

Figure 4 Specific spider diagram

——— Talk priorities through ———

If you suddenly decide to change the priorities in your life at work or at home, other people are going to notice. If at work you suddenly decide that financial projects are going to take precedence over reports from now on, your staff will want to know why. Or, if after years of preferring to play golf or tennis on a Sunday morning, you announce that you'd prefer to take your family to the beach, your partner will want to know why.

If you want to keep on track with your aims, you have to let other people know what you are doing. Apart from anything else, you will need their co-operation to succeed. You can only do so much yourself. (See Chapter 10 for more on empowering your staff.)

Explaining to your staff that your aim from now on is to improve the financial standing of your section will inspire them to help you, rather than hinder you by trying to continue the old system. And explaining to your partner that you have decided to spend more time with your family (one of your life's goals) will stop worries about illness (or madness!). However much you want to spring a new changed you onto an unsuspecting world, it is better not to. Tell other people what you are up to so that they can help you.

You do not have to tell them what your goals are but it can be helpful to tell them what your immediate objectives are. They may even be able to suggest areas of your life that you might have overlooked. Perhaps you have ignored an important aspect of your accounts system or have forgotten about your secret desire to climb Everest, for example. By talking to others you will get a more rounded picture of yourself and your aims.

Only by visualising your own future can you see what you need to do to get there. You may not achieve all of the things that you want to, but by aiming for them you will achieve more than if you had no goals at all.

TOP TEN TIPS

1 Decide what you really want from life.
2 Don't be afraid of aiming for the stars.
3 Use the 80/20 rule to decide what is important.
4 Remember you can achieve great things by taking small steps.
5 Define your goals and objectives in each area of your life.
6 Make your objectives attainable, measurable and positive.
7 Prioritise your goals and objectives.
8 In an emergency, prioritise quickly.
9 Use spider diagrams to free your thoughts.
10 Don't waste time on activities that don't contribute to your goals.

Summary

To get the most from your life you need to imitate successful people and visualise how you want your life to be. Remember that the 80/20 rule means that you should spend the productive 20 per cent of your time working towards your goals. Start taking control by defining the key areas of your life and deciding what you want to achieve in them. Write down your main goals and break these down into manageable objectives and achievable steps. Timetable these objectives and steps into your days. If you find working out your goals hard, use spider diagrams to free your thoughts. Don't be afraid of visualising goals that you only dream about.

2

HOW MUCH TIME HAVE YOU GOT?

In this chapter you will find out how much time you spend on your activities and how to reappraise the way you use your time. By the end of the chapter you will know exactly how you use your time now and how to decide what you really want to do with it.

—— Do you know what you do? ——

It is easy for me to say 'Reorganise the way you use your time and you will become more effective and efficient'. But how can you do so unless you know exactly what you do with it now?

I expect you know more or less what you do with your time for each day of the week. For example, you can tell me that on Saturday you get up, have breakfast, go shopping, visit your aunt Jemima, have lunch, go swimming, have supper, go to the cinema and go to bed. But can you tell me how much time you spend on each of those activities? And what about all the smaller things that fill your day, for example reading the papers, having coffee, chatting with friends – can you remember what they were and how much time you spent on them?

You only have the same amount of time in a day as we all do – 24 hours. Until you know exactly what you do with that 24 hours you cannot work out where you can reorganise and save time. The only way to find out what you really do all day, and how long you spend on it, is to keep a time log.

Keeping a time log

A time log is an account of how you spend your time each day. The easiest way to keep one is to write down the starting and finishing time of everything you do from the time you get up to the time you go to bed. So your log might look like this:

- 7.00 got up
- 7.05 shower
- 7.10 clean teeth and get dressed
- 7.20 breakfast
- 7.45 left for work
- 8.30 at work
- 8.35 coffee & newspaper
- 8.50 letters, etc.

If recording your day in such detail is too time consuming, write down roughly when you started each activity and how long you spent on it, for example, Shower – approx. 7.30 – 5 mins. Obviously, the former more detailed log will be more helpful but any indication of how you spend your time will be useful.

Don't forget to include seemingly 'dead' time or trivial activities, such as eating snacks, chats, phone calls, reading.

You don't need to keep a log like this every day for a fortnight, as some people suggest. You haven't got time; nor have most people. A couple of days will be enough. If you keep an office diary you can work out your time log for a few days from that to supplement the detailed logs.

However you keep the time log, try to be as honest as possible. Include everything you do, however trivial. Unless you are honest you cannot see where your time goes.

At work include phone calls, appointments, interruptions, meetings, dealing with paperwork, projects, writing, planning time, plus all the minor activities that make up your working day.

Make comments against each entry. Describe how you felt about it, how effective it was, whether it contributed to one of your goals, how it could be improved.

Your time balance sheet

Another way of looking at your use of time is to work out how much time you have left at the end of a typical week. It works like this:

No of hours in the week		168
Sleeping	−56	112
Eating	−10.5	101.5
Washing, dressing, etc.	− 3.5	98
Working	−40	58
Watching TV	−14	44
Commuting	− 5	39
Reading	−10	29
Family activities	−15	14
Time with partner	− 8	6
Religion	− 8	− 2
Personal business/errands/shopping	− 4	− 6
Hobbies/interests	−10	−16
Wasted or 'dead' time,	− 2.5	−18.5
e.g. waiting for meetings,		
travelling		

As you can see it is easy to use up more time than you actually have! Of course, some activities will overlap but you get a clear idea of where the bulk of your time goes and can see where it can be saved.

Can you, for instance, get up an hour earlier or spend less time reading or watching TV?

TIME MANAGEMENT TIP

Don't reduce your sleep time if you get eight hours' sleep or less – you will be too tired to work properly. Why not reduce time on watching TV instead?

—— Prime time or wasted time? ——

Now that you have a few days of a time log in front of you, work out how long you spend on each activity. Some of the time will be spent on things that you cannot avoid, which are vital to your life, for example, sleeping, eating, toiletries, dressing, getting to work. Other commitments you will choose for yourself, for example going to church, attending evening class, regular sport. Some activities will be imposed on you, such as work commitments, or caring for a relative. Yet more activities will be things that you can take or leave, for example chatting to a friend, reading the papers, going to the cinema.

What you are looking for is a balance between what you must do and what you want to do. But first you must calculate how much time you spend on each activity. You will probably be surprised at how much time is taken up by trivial things. Or by how much of your day is spent on maintenance tasks, such as shopping and eating.

Peter, a shop manager, kept a time log and discovered that at work he spent too much time in his office doing paperwork and not enough time with his staff. After work he spent more time in front of the TV or at the pub than with his family. By reducing his paperwork (as described in Chapter 7) he was able to keep a closer eye on his staff and sort out problems before they got out of hand. At home he reduced the time he spent watching TV and limited his trips to the pub to twice a week. He saw more of his family and was happier – and healthier!

Saving time

There are three ways to save time once you know how you spend it. You can eliminate or change some of the activities; you can reduce the time taken over them; or you can rearrange them to make better use of the time. In practice, you will want to use a combination of all three.

First, mark all the activities you do that are time wasting – that extra cup of coffee before you start work; reading that irrelevant magazine; talking to Fred in the next office for half an hour, and so on. All these activities could be eliminated entirely. If you can't bring yourself to cut out unnecessary activities in one go, then ease yourself into it. Take that cup of coffee to your desk and drink it while you start work; save the magazine as a treat for the end of the day; have an occasional lunch with Fred and a long chat over it.

TIME MANAGEMENT TIP

Keep a note of the change you are making in your diary. Tick it every day when you have done it – that way you reinforce the habit.

Eliminating all time-wasting activities does not mean that you should eliminate all non-work activities. Your leisure time is important for relaxation and recuperation. Just ensure that it takes place out of work hours and that the leisure activities you choose are ones that you really want to do. Taking a tap-dancing evening class is no fun if you are only doing it to keep fit. Going swimming or playing tennis to keep fit might suit you better, while you take a line-dancing class for fun.

Changing your activities is part of time management practice, as I have shown you. If you are filling your time with activities that do not help your work or contribute to your own personal life goals, why do them? If you are doing too many unproductive things, then find a different way of doing them or eliminate them.

Jill, an advertising executive, found that she was spending more time wining and dining clients than working on accounts. Her creative skills were being used less and less. She knew that meeting clients was important and that a meal was often the best way to do so. She decided to set strict time limits to the meals and, when due to meet one client on two occasions, to send her assistant for the second. That way she cut her meal dates by half but still flattered the clients by turning up for the first meal. Her assistant also benefited by more experience of dealing with clients.

Check your use of time

Here is another way to discover how much time you are spending on unimportant activities that contribute little to your day.

Take your diary or timetable for a week and some coloured pens. Choose a different colour for each type of activity. Use a red pen to highlight all unimportant activities or wasted time. If your diary has a lot of red in it, you are wasting a lot of time. See if you can eliminate some of this 'red' time. Next, rearrange your activities so that like activities are grouped together. This is a more efficient use of your time. So, for example, you would do all your letter writing in one half hour in the morning instead of ten minutes in the morning and 20 minutes in the afternoon.

If you get a page with different colours on every line then your work is fragmented. However, if the result is broad bands of colour then you are already managing to consolidate your work and group like activities together.

How much time do you control?

Your time log will show you how much of your time you have at your command. Mark all the occasions that you were interrupted by other people, whether by visits or phone calls. How much of your work was dictated by other people's priorities? Once you know this you can take steps to ensure that your priorities prevail. Take steps to stop this unproductive use of your time. (See Chapter 8 to control your phone calls.)

If you really want more time – be ruthless

It is no good being feeble about working through your time log and making changes where you can. If you really want to save time then something must go or be changed. Work through your time log and see where changes can be made. That way you will get an overall picture of what you need to do.

If you don't think you can make all the changes at once (and that requires the kind of superhuman determination that most of us haven't got) then make one change a day or a week. By gradually introducing the changes your life will improve over time and you will not worry about how to do it.

The urgent/important matrix

You can make decisions about the use of your time by deciding whether it is important or unimportant, urgent or non-urgent and their combinations. The matrix looks like this:

	URGENT	NON-URGENT
IMPORTANT		
UNIMPORTANT		

Look at each activity and decide whether it was:

- important and urgent
- important but non-urgent
- unimportant but urgent
- unimportant and non-urgent.

You need to deal with these in different ways and their priority will depend on this. If the work is important and urgent you need to make this a top priority and deal with it straight away. An example might be writing a speech for the chairman's delivery the same evening. The task might be important but non-urgent, such as a long-term project. In that case, you would timetable it for a future period while still allowing time for its completion. If something is urgent but not important, such as getting a memo out to colleagues within 24 hours of a meeting, you could delegate it to a member of staff or allow time after the first priorities to do it. Remember that if someone else gives you work and tells you it is urgent, that is their view of its priority. And finally, if the task is unimportant and non-urgent, why do it at all?

	URGENT	NON-URGENT
IMPORTANT	*Do it now!*	*Timetable it for later*
UNIMPORTANT	*Delegate or do it later*	*Don't do it!*

If you have looked at your time log and worked out which of the matrix choices your tasks have fallen into, you can see how much of your day is spent concentrating on unimportant activities. When you have new tasks, ask yourself where they come in the matrix and allocate time for them accordingly. You will find that you will be concentrating on the important things that help you reach your goals.

Habit helps

Some habits are bad, but most are good because they give us a routine and make getting through life easier and quicker. Most people have a routine for getting up and out of the house in the morning, for example. If we didn't we would be slowed down considerably by having to consciously work out each day what we had to do. With our clothes ready, car keys always in the same place, the breakfast table set, we can get out of the house in a few minutes if we have to.

The best way of introducing a new way of working into your life is to build it into your routines. If you want to stop wasting time while drinking that early morning coffee at work, for example, then consciously take it to your desk tomorrow and get straight on with opening your post. You will have to think about it for a few days and even have to work consciously at it for a few days after that, but then it will become a habit.

It takes three or four weeks to create a habit. Some minor things, such as the coffee, may take less time to become ingrained, but others, such as writing up your diary each night or changing the way you deal with phone calls, will take longer. Decide what you need to change and do it every day. If you lapse, don't give up. Just start again the next day making a conscious effort to get it right. As time goes on it will get easier.

TIME MANAGEMENT TIP

Ask a friend to remind you when you are lapsing into time-wasting habits.

Ratio of goals to time

What your time log will show you is how much of your time is spent on things that help you reach the goals you set for yourself in Chapter 1. If you find that few of your activities are helping you achieve these goals, then you need to rethink your life. For example, there is no reason why you should not want to climb Everest, but are any of your activities helping you achieve this goal? If not, what can you do about it? Perhaps you could cancel the usual Thursday evening session at the pub with your friends and enrol on a climbing course at the local college. Or you could substitute a book on climbing for the magazine you look through on Saturdays. These are only small things, but they are a start.

Obviously some goals are more important than others. If you have put work goals at the forefront of your ambitions, then you will concentrate on introducing changes that contribute to those goals. Only you can decide what ratio the goals in your life should have.

Targets for your time

Now that you know how you spend your time you can see what uses of it you are not happy about and decide what your preferred use of it should be. You will, of course, have to take into account the demands of your job and home life. So, you should first write down what your job description is – what exactly is expected of you at work and at home. Within these restrictions, decide what you want to achieve in the remaining time. Refer to the goals at the front of your diary. Set realistic targets for use of your time.

Work out the real cost in terms of whether it is valuable to you according to your defined work or main goals.

To make more effective use of your time, batch similar and routine jobs together. Whenever you have to do anything, write it in your timetable so that you don't have to think about it, it is already scheduled.

Try to allow blocks of time for getting on with longer projects. An hour and a half is about right. This gives you enough time to get something worthwhile done but does not tax your powers of concentration.

— Unimportant but good for you? —

In spite of what I have said about making sure that you do things that are important for your life goals, there are some things that may not seem important in general but which are good for you. Sport is one of them. Concern for your health should be an integral part of your life. But quite often we do not rate sport highly among our activities.

However, it should be one of our concerns. You do not have to be obsessive about it but you should build some form of healthy activity into your daily/weekly routine.

Most people have not taken part in any sport since they left school. In fact, for many, sport ended after compulsory education. But we are now more aware of the benefits of a healthy lifestyle and sport has been shown to improve this greatly.

You do not need to be good at sport to enjoy it, nor good at team games. There are many ways you can build sport in a wide sense into your life – walking to work, yoga, swimming, cycling, dancing are all good healthy activities. Choose one that you enjoy so that you do not mind doing it regularly.

Don't forget your mental health too. Activities that can keep you alert include:

- doing crosswords
- reading a book
- reading newspapers
- relaxing quietly
- taking time to pursue a hobby or interest
- visiting friends
- taking a holiday.

None of these things is important in itself; most of them do not contribute to our efficiency at work and of course they do take up some of your time. But everybody needs to do some things for pleasure and relaxation alone. Without some pleasures in life and the chance to expand your mind and relate to other people away from the pressures of work, you can become ill and stressed. You do not have to spend a disproportionate amount of time on leisure activities but they are life-enhancers. People who build these into their lives return to the workplace happier and more relaxed, and work better because of it.

Take a holiday

Don't be like many workers today and avoid taking your holidays on the grounds that 'They can't do without me' or 'If I take time off I'll never catch up'. First, if you don't take a holiday you are likely to end up ill and have to take time off anyway – not to mention the strain it will put on your family life. Second, if you follow the time management ideas in this book you will not need to 'catch up' – or if you do you can do so quickly. Finally, you are not indispensable. If you dropped dead tonight the world would not come to a halt even if it did inconvenience a few people and upset your loved ones. Take that holiday and return to the fray refreshed and invigorated.

TIME MANAGEMENT TIP

Book your holidays in advance, if possible. Mark them in your diary or timetable at the beginning of the year. That way you have no excuse for avoiding them.

How do you want to spend your time?

You've recorded your time log and worked out how much of your time you spend on wasteful activities. Now comes the fun bit. You have to decide what you do want to do with your time.

Certain things are always going to be part of your day. You have to sleep, eat, wash, dress and get to work. But you have a choice about other things. Do you want to see more of your family and friends? Do you want to take up a new hobby? Do you want to involve yourself more in the community? Do you want to get promotion or change your job?

The life goals you worked out after reading Chapter 1 will show you what you want out of life. Now you have to narrow it down a bit more. How do you want to spend the next year? The next six months? Your week? Each day? Sit down for a few minutes and close your eyes. Picture yourself during the perfect day. What would you be doing first thing in the morning? How would you spend your time at work? What would your evenings be like? Who would you see and talk to? Then do the same for the week.

Now list some of the most important differences between your perfect day and your present day. Look at it carefully. Can you make any changes to your present day to bring it closer to your ideal?

Suppose, for example, that your perfect day included getting into work at 10 a.m., getting through your work quickly, having a long lunch, leaving work early and spending the evening having dinner with your partner. In reality however, you get into work at 8.30 a.m., spend the day snowed under with work and snatch a sandwich to eat at your desk for lunch, spend the evening catching up with paperwork after a quick supper, and only have time to chat to your partner for half an hour before going to bed. This is not an unusual scenario. How can you bring your working day and perfect day closer together?

First, put into practice some of the time management techniques in this book. That way you can get on top of your work and free up your lunch-times and evenings. As you get more effective at work, you could ask your boss if you could work a flexible week allowing you to start later some days. Finally, you could arrange to meet your partner once a week near your workplace for that meal.

Your real day won't yet be your perfect day, though you will have made changes that bring it closer to your ideal. But unless you know what your ideal is, you can't aim for it.

—— Turning dreams into reality ——

If you don't have dreams, you can't make them come true. The higher we aim in life, the closer we get to achieving what we want to. And even if we don't succeed we reach a few peaks on the way. Our lives become more fulfilled just by trying.

TOP TEN TIPS

1 Keep a time log – be honest!
2 Highlight wasted time.
3 Work out how much time you control – aim to increase it.
4 Prioritise using the important/unimportant, urgent/non-urgent matrix.
5 Turn good practices into habits.

---

6 If you return to time-wasting ways, start again.
7 Take all your holidays.
8 Use some time to improve your mental and physical health.
9 If something won't help you reach your goals, don't do it.
10 Aim to make your actual day like your dream day.

Summary

Before you can plan your days you need to know how much time you spend on each activity. Keep a time log for a few days – ideally a fortnight. Be honest and include all the minor activities that make up your day. When you know exactly how long you spend on everything, you can see which activities to eliminate and how to plan your time. When you plan your timetable, remember to include some leisure time and health activities.

3

PLAN YOUR TIME

This chapter describes time management tools, their advantages and disadvantages and how to use them effectively. It explains how to plan your time for maximum effectiveness and reminds you of the importance of family and personal time.

—— Take time to make time ——

Most time management gurus or books will tell you to manage all your time by using a diary or planner. They may recommend something so complex that the average person will spend half their time filling it in. Some will encourage you to keep several of these on the go at once – one for home, one for the office and one for your briefcase or bag. This can cause problems. Louisa, a sales director, kept a desk diary, home diary and handbag diary until one day she booked an important meeting with clients in her handbag diary at a time she had marked in her desk diary to give a major presentation to the board, because she hadn't co-ordinated the two diaries.

If you are clear about your objectives, you can plan your time on practically anything – a scrap of paper, a notebook, a simple diary, a complex diary or the full page planner. Ideally, keep your plans, timetables, diary and notes in one place. You may need a complex and large planner to do this but it is possible to keep everything in one diary – it depends on what your needs are and how you work. Choose a diary or planner large enough to contain many sections – the basic daily diary as well as space for notes and to-do lists – but small enough to carry in a briefcase or even a large coat pocket. I keep my time management priorities of work, family, study and leisure in a basic A5 week-to-view diary from the local office supplies store.

Your time planner choices are:

- loose paper
- notebook
- diary
- time management planner
- electronic organiser
- computer.

Advantages and disadvantages of time management tools

If you know your priorities and have a good memory (or a good secretary) you might be able to keep everything you need to plan your day on a scrap of paper. But most of us need more than that. A diary is a good start. You probably recognise two kinds of diary: the kind to record your innermost thoughts and the appointment diary. For many people, a diary is just a place for noting down appointments and phone numbers: it is not used for serious planning.

A time management diary has the days divided into times in at least half-hourly sections. If you are a very busy person, choose one with divisions into 15 or 20 minute slots. (See Figure 5.) It should also have pages for notes and a daily section for lists and notes. Whether you choose a week-to-view or day-to-view will be up to you, but if you choose a daily diary you may need to refer back frequently to a weekly plan.

In a diary there may be extra sections for:

- personal details
- notes
- general information
- expenses
- road/rail maps.

DATE:

7.00		5.15	
7.15		5.30	
7.30		5.45	
7.45		6.00	
8.00		6.15	
8.15		6.30	
8.30		6.45	
8.45		7.00	
9.00		7.15	
9.15		7.30	
9.30		7.45	
9.45		8.00	
10.00		✓ X	To Do List
10.15			
10.30			
10.45			
11.00			
11.15			
11.30			
11.45			
12.00			
12.15			
12.30			
12.45			
1.00			
1.15			
1.30			
1.45		☎	Phone calls
2.00			
2.15			
2.30			
2.45			
3.00			
3.15			
3.30			
3.45			
4.00			
4.15			
4.30			
4.45			
5.00			
	Notes		Notes

Figure 5 Diary page example

If some pages in standard diaries are irrelevant for your needs, take a tip from Pete, a computer analyst. He has a favourite type of diary but it has some irrelevant pages. He tears these out so that he can focus on the essential information.

You may use a notebook for keeping notes and making to-do lists. But if you keep it separate from your diary or planner you may lose it or forget to refer to it. If you forget your diary or planner when you are out and about, make notes on paper and then transfer them immediately into your diary when you get back to the office or home. Many managers prefer a two-page-a-day diary so that they have plenty of space for notes opposite each day.

In a time planner you need:

- daily time sheets
- weekly plan sheets
- monthly plan sheets
- year planner chart
- note pages
- to-do list pages.

Management planner

Many busy people use a management planner. This is a combination of a diary with daily time markings, weekly planning sheets, monthly planning sheets, a year chart and pages and spaces for to-do lists and notes. It is comprehensive and effective if used properly. Many people find that their lives are transformed by keeping track of their time needs in one comprehensive volume. The disadvantage is that it can be a bulky book, which can make it less useful for making notes on the move.

Be ruthless about discarding used or useless pages, otherwise your planner will get fatter and you will lose track of vital notes among the pages. You will become discouraged about organising your time if you see your planner expanding – a slim planner means a happy time manager!

TIME MANAGEMENT TIP

Use a loose-leaf planner. You can then move your notes and lists close to the relevant page without rewriting them.

Electronic organiser

The electronic organiser is the epitome of a planning tool because everything you need is in one place and it is small enough to carry everywhere. It will usually contain an appointments listing, sometimes with automatic insertions of specified regular appointments, addresses and phone numbers, electronic communications, word-processing, to-do lists, spreadsheets and graphs. With the addition of a modem, an electronic organiser can send and receive faxes and e-mail, so it is possible to keep your appointments diary right up to date by contact with your office. You can also print the information in your organiser onto paper or transfer the information straight onto your desktop publishing computer.

Electronic organisers:

- keep you in touch when away from home and office
- are portable
- contain powerful computer programs.

However, there are disadvantages. Unless the organiser has sufficient memory it can only keep the minimum of information in any section. So there may be room for phone numbers but not addresses, for example, or only brief indications of your appointments. You cannot see more than one page at a time on an electronic organiser, which some people find irritating. You can, however, flip from one page to another. The screens on organisers are very small so if your eyesight is poor the screen may be difficult to read. You can use one for taking notes but a piece of paper and a pen is quicker and less obtrusive in a meeting and you are not looking down on a screen instead of at the speaker. You have to recharge batteries frequently and could possibly run out of power when you need the organiser most. On the whole, electronic organisers are good for daily appointments but less useful for long-term planning. Larger computers may also have planning diaries programmed in but these are not portable and are therefore only useful for office-based work.

John, a company director, thinks his new electronic organiser is the most effective way of planning his time. 'I used to keep an office diary and a small personal diary in my jacket. My organiser eliminates the need for both of these. Appointments, addresses, notes, everything goes straight into my organiser. I can send the information straight onto my secretary's computer so we are both up to date with my movements. I can even use it to send and receive faxes and e-mail. I plug it into the recharger at work so the battery seldom, if ever, runs out. It is an ideal size because I can carry it in my pocket or briefcase so it goes with me everywhere.'

—— What is the diary/planner for? ——

Your diary must contain everything that you will need to plan your life, from the main objectives and goals you defined in Chapter 1 to how many meetings you have on a particular Thursday afternoon. From how much time you can spend on your leisure pursuits to when you can visit that elderly aunt. Your diary should contain:

- your life goals
- the objectives for achieving these goals
- steps to achieving the objectives
- daily tasks.

Relate each of these needs to the main areas of your life, for example:

- work
- family
- leisure
- study
- other.

Remember that planning your life will be easier if you keep everything in one place. It will also enable you to take an overview of your time.

—— Planning by priorities ——

As you worked through Chapter 1, you decided what your main life goals are and the steps you need to take to achieve them. In Chapter 2, you discovered what you really do with your time. You have also chosen your preferred diary or planner. Now put these together to plan your life.

TIME MANAGEMENT TIP

Write your life goals at the front of your planner and read them every day to inspire you and focus your priorities.

Remember to arrange everything according to your priorities. So, if you are deciding between several uses of your time, make the choice that helps you reach one of your main goals. For example, if you have a couple of spare hours on a summer Saturday lunch time you might have to choose between going to the pub with some friends or taking your family on a picnic in the country. If one of your goals in life is to spend more time with your family, then go on the picnic. If you are lucky, you may be able to combine several priorities in one activity.

Fixed times

Everybody has some regular uses of their time that they cannot alter. Business people may have meetings, presentations, visits, and so on, which are fixed. Other people may have evening classes, school visits, voluntary work, sports fixtures that shape their lives. Write your fixed times in your planner first. (In later chapters I will show you how to reduce the amount of time you need to spend on meetings.) Write them in your yearly planner, then your monthly planner and then at the exact time in your daily planner. Record fixed times in your out-of-work hours such as voluntary work, evening classes or collecting children from school. Now see what time you have free. Allocate sections for work and leisure according to your priorities. Work from the yearly planner to the daily one. Divide large jobs into small sections and fit this in with your daily and monthly routine.

Using checklists

It is easy to allocate fixed items but more difficult to decide what to do on a monthly or daily basis so that you work effectively but have plenty of time in which to do it. Make a list of everything you need to do to complete each piece of work. So, if you have to arrange a conference, the time of the conference, can go down in your yearly planner. Time allocated for contacting participants and ordering stationery could go into the monthly planner. Then decide which weeks are suitable for the jobs you need to do, such as confirming the printing, booking the hall, etc. Finally, in your day planner, allocate time for preparing the conference blurb, collecting the printed material and talking to visual aids technicians.

Estimating time

Now that you have worked out what you want to achieve and the steps you need to take to achieve it, you need to work out how long each step will take. Don't try to work this out exactly; make an educated guess. So, perhaps you will write down:

1 Prepare for conference (two weeks).
2 Reorganise B section (six months).
3 Get brochures printed (five weeks).

Fit these periods of time into your calendar. You can then see immediately where you are going to be too busy and can rearrange your schedule accordingly. Once you have worked out the overall picture you can do the same with smaller blocks of time, such as months and weeks. So, for example, your weekly list might read:

1 Get sales figures from Janet (15 minutes).
2 Write introduction to report (half an hour).
3 Write main body of report (one hour).
4 Dictate letters (20 minutes).
5 Meeting with boss (half an hour).

Fit these periods of time into your diary in a suitable order. Write in some spare time each day and week, too. This allows you to be more flexible and to make last-minute arrangements if necessary.

Don't worry about trying to put exact times in. You will over- or under-estimate at first. As you have more experience of the system, you will get better at estimating the time needed for each job.

TIME MANAGEMENT TIP

When estimating time for a long-term project, work backwards from the deadline. That way you can make sure that all parts of the project fit into the time available and are completed on time.

Where do you start?

You might have defined your goals but don't know which one to start working towards. Choose the one that would make the most difference to your life quickly. Suppose that one of your goals is to be chief executive and aiming for that would transform your work practices. You should choose that goal to start with and fit the objectives into your timetable. Add objectives and tasks for other goals in order of your priorities.

By prioritising your goals you give a sense of order to your life.

It is useful to make 'to-do' lists for the jobs in our lives. These will help you to break down large tasks into smaller ones, so that you can allocate time more effectively. To-do lists can cover yearly, monthly, weekly or daily periods. Prepare daily to-do lists the night before or first thing in the morning and list everything you have to accomplish during the day. Don't just work through the list completing each item in turn, or you will never get the main work done. Prioritise your list into three categories:

1 Must be done.
2 Should be done.
3 It would be nice if it gets done.

See what time you have free after your fixed appointments, then make a realistic daily 'to-do' list based on the time available.

TIME MANAGEMENT TIP

Don't try to prioritise lists as you go along. Write the items as you think of them and prioritise them afterwards.

Work through your list doing all the 'ones' first, then as many 'twos' as possible. Finally, if you have time, do some 'threes' but don't worry if you don't get to them. By working with lists this way you will get the important work done first. If you don't complete everything on your list by the end of the day, carry uncompleted tasks over to the next day's list. (See Figure 6.)

Prioritising in an emergency

Under normal circumstances you will have time to evaluate each piece of work as you are given it and to allocate it a priority. You can prioritise the papers that land on your desk (in Chapter 7 I explain in

Phone John about new project schedule	1
Give presentation to board	1
Write to Sam R. - enclose latest report	3
Team meeting - ask Tony for information on XYZ co.	2
Send printouts to Charles	3
Phone Terry to arrange next meeting	3
Phone Betty re participants for Monday's meeting	2
Alan's appraisal - remember to ask Barry to sit in	1
Buy theatre tickets on way home	3
Recall documents for major project	1

Figure 6 Daily to-do list example

more detail how to deal with the daily round of paper) but suppose your in-tray is constantly full, or you have a sudden influx of work. If you cannot deal with the workload reasonably quickly you will become stressed and burnt out.

If you do find yourself in this situation, don't panic. Quickly sort your papers into four piles according to when the work needs to be done, for example, to be dealt with:

- immediately
- in a few days' time
- next week
- next month.

Quickly prioritise any other work in the same way. That way you have a basic plan for getting through the work. Start with the work to be done immediately, then do the next pile, and so on.

This rough and ready system is for when everything gets on top of you and quickly puts you back in command of the situation. Once you have reduced this overload you can once again organise how you deal with work and paper more effectively.

Weekly project page

The most important part of good time management is the weekly project page and daily to-do list. The weekly project page is the 'what I want to do' list for the coming week. At the top, list your objectives for the week in order of priority. Keep it to no more than you can reasonably handle – three is a good number. Underneath this, list all the steps you need to take to achieve each of these objectives and then prioritise each set of objectives. Next to them, write down the approximate amount of time you think each will take and on what day of the week you expect to do it. (See Figure 7). Now you know what you need to do and when you can fit these into your daily schedules around your fixed times. When estimating time for tasks, try not to allow either too much, or too little time. If you allow too much, you will simply find the work to fill it; if you allow too little, you will be forced to finish the task at another time. You will have some idea of how long tasks take from having completed the time log as recommended in Chapter 2. As you become more efficient you will get better at estimating the amount of time you need.

Complete project	1		
Prepare presentation for Friday	2		
Get brochure ready for printing	3		
Project – Tuesday	– ask Gary to send latest documents	2	5 mins
	– get reports from finance dept.	2	10 mins
	– agree timetable with Celia	1	15 mins
	– write introduction	1	1 hour
– Thursday	– write first section	1	1 hr 30 mins
	– check introduction	2	20 mins
– Friday	– write second section	1	1 hr
	– check first section	2	30 mins
Presentation to board (for Friday)			
	– check notes	2	30 mins
	– prepare overheads	1	1 hr 30 mins
	– run through presentation	1	45 mins
	– advance copy to Peter	2	(Sheila)
Brochures – Friday – check proofs	1		1 hour
– instruct printer	2		30 mins
– complete distribution list	2		15 mins

Figure 7 Weekly project list example

Daily to-do lists

When you start each day you will have a list of things to do as the day goes on. Some of these will have been carried over from the day before and some you will add during the day. Fill in these tasks in the remaining times of the day, using your objectives for the week and your main goals as a guide. Remember your matrix from Chapter 2, and judge the tasks according to whether they have a deadline and must be done, or are important as well as urgent. These must have priority in your daily timetable.

Don't forget to:

- fill in large blocks of time for important steps
- change your timetable around to accommodate high-priority tasks
- allow extra time for unexpected events.

Reducing non-essential time

When you have filled in your diary or planner according to these lists, you will see that previously a lot of your time was filled with dealing with non-essential activities, such as having a cup of coffee and chatting to your friends or reading articles in a business magazine.

I will tell you how to deal with many major time-wasting habits later in the book, but you can start by working out what your non-essential time is used for. Suppose, for example, you spend a lot of time reading interesting but non-essential articles in the two magazines you are sent each week at work. Solve this by tearing out or photocopying those articles and putting them in your briefcase to read at home. If you can't live without that cup of coffee and the chat with your friends, have it at the beginning of your lunch break while eating your sandwich.

When you have worked out what the non-essential activities are, try to eliminate them, combine them, or do them at a time that will not interfere with your main prioritised activities.

Allow time for recuperation

Many managers are so keen on the idea of planning their time that they do not allow for relaxation and recuperation. It is possible to plan your day so that you are active for every moment from the time you wake up to the time you go to bed. This is not a good use of your time.

Nobody works at their best non-stop. Everybody needs some time to themselves, often somewhere quiet on their own. You need this to gather your strength, to relax and calm yourself and to recover your energy. If you don't allow for this in your day you will become stressed and ill, and less effective.

You will have a different way of relaxing from me or your colleagues. I like to read a book, go for a walk or do a crossword. You may prefer aerobics, watching television or meditation. However you relax, plan it into your day. A busy manager could take 20 minutes in an empty boardroom to read a book or simply sit and think. Don't neglect this important part of your day.

When to fill in your planner

As soon as you know about a fixed appointment, put it into your diary or planner straight away. At the beginning of the year, fill in as much of your diary as possible and amend it monthly and weekly according to your priorities at that time. Fill in the daily diary and lists at the beginning of each day or last thing at night.

——— Allow for emergencies ———

Don't think that if you plan your day it is fixed and immutable and that spontaneity becomes difficult. Planning your day allows you to be prepared for emergencies or changes of plan.

With a disorganised system you may have to do everything if an emergency arises and then catch up with work late at night. With a planned day you can see immediately where to allocate time for work you are doing because you know what has to be done and when. If this worries you, plan a free hour into your day that can be filled or not, or moved as circumstances dictate.

Crisis management

The worst emergency you can have is when a problem turns into a crisis. This is where time planning comes into its own. When a crisis occurs you can immediately put work aside or delegate it, knowing that you have planned some leeway into your day.

In a crisis, time is vital; you need to get your responses to your boss and staff and possibly the press, public and shareholders as quickly as possible in order to reduce the worst consequences. To do this, make sure that you have a contingency plan ready for an emergency. Plan ahead so that everyone knows their responsibilities when a crisis occurs. Keep a look out for warning of a possible crisis so that you are ready to put your contingency plan into action if necessary.

Make sure that your contingency plan includes:

- who will deal with what work
- what kinds of work can be ignored or deferred until the crisis is over
- who will undertake specific actions
- prepared sample responses covering various types of crisis
- emergency phone, fax and e-mail numbers
- who will deal with the press and public (if necessary).

As well as having a contingency plan for a crisis, know how to deal with it so that you do not waste time wondering how to respond:

1 React quickly.
2 Don't overreact.
3 Watch out for anyone taking advantage of the crisis.
4 Admit any fault.
5 Explain what will happen now.
6 Don't assume everyone will be antagonistic.
7 Be ready to talk and answer questions about the crisis.
8 Call on any goodwill you have built up.

By planning ahead you can make the best use of your time in an emergency. Your diary or planner will enable you to see at a glance what needs to be dealt with so that you can quickly replan it and delegate where necessary.

TIME-PLANNING TIPS

1 Write down fixed appointments.
2 Break down major tasks into smaller jobs.
3 Allocate jobs according to your goals and objectives.
4 Don't crowd appointments and other allocated times into a short period.
5 Make weekly project lists and daily to-do plans.
6 Prioritise your lists.
7 Carry items over to the next list if necessary.
8 Build in recuperation time.
9 Have a contingency plan for a crisis.

Summary

Choose the time management tool you are happy with. Record your fixed appointments and then prioritise your other commitments as they occur. Prepare daily, weekly and monthly to-do lists. Fill in a yearly planner. Remember to include family and personal time.

Time management frees time for your priorities and makes you more effective at work. By planning your time in advance using the time management tool you prefer, you can fit more into your life at work and home and still have time for leisure and pleasure. Effective time management keeps you in command of your day but is flexible enough to accommodate emergencies.

4

USING
TRANSITION TIME

This chapter explains what transition time is and how you can use it productively. It covers how to eliminate normally unproductive time and what to do with the bits and pieces of spare time left over. After reading this chapter you will always have something to do in a spare ten minutes.

What is transition time?

Have you ever sat waiting for a doctor's or dentist's appointment? Do you ever travel to work on public transport? Have people ever arrived late for a meeting with you? Do you ever find yourself with ten or fifteen minutes to spare between appointments?

All these are common examples of transition time, or 'dead' time, the odd pieces of time between everything you do. These valuable extra bits of time are often 'transition' because people think that they are too short to do anything with. They are often squandered by hanging about.

Transition time also includes time that you spend on preparatory activities, such as washing and dressing or getting organised to go out. You are doing something, but the time is transition because not all of it is being used productively.

Used sensibly, these time slots can be filled productively. If used creatively they can not only reduce your main workload but can save you time overall on your working day.

— When are your transition times? —

To use transition times effectively you need to know when yours usually occur. Sit down with your time log from Chapter 2 and see where the bits of spare time in your day occur. Make a note of them and how long they last. Look also for times when you are travelling or doing other unproductive activities. Add up these times and you will be surprised at how much of your day is spent unproductively.

Examples of transition times are:

- journey to and from work
- between arrival and starting work
- between meetings
- waiting for people to arrive
- waiting for appointments
- lunch time (perhaps)
- slack time at conferences
- holidays (perhaps)
- during breakfast
- evenings at home (perhaps).

Your list will probably have other occasions, too. But the common theme is that all of these bits of time are usually not used, or only used for non-productive purposes.

Notice that for some examples I have put 'perhaps' afterwards. That is because you *can* use those times for work but you might not be popular with your family if you do so. And using your lunch break is not sensible if it is your only chance of a break during the day. You will not be productive if you are tired and hungry.

TIME MANAGEMENT TIP

Use your lunch break to have a healthy meal and a short walk outdoors. You will feel more energetic and alert during the afternoon and will be more productive.

—— Dealing with transition time ——

Your plan of action for transition time starts by working out how to reduce it or use it more constructively. There are four main steps:

1 Reduce unproductive time where possible.
2 Do two or more things at once.
3 Find a quiet place or create a solitude 'shield'.
4 Have a specific plan for transition time.

Reducing unproductive time

Before you decide what to do with any 'spare' time, see if you can reduce unproductive time. Can you rearrange meetings so that you do not have long waiting times between them? Can you find a quicker route to work? Reduce any 'wasted' time as much as possible.

Here are some examples of time you might save each week:

- cut down on washing and dressing each morning by 15 mins (1 hour 45 minutes)
- watch half an hour less TV every day (3 hours 30 minutes)
- avoid unnecessary meetings (3 hours)
- cut down on coffee breaks (1 hour)
- decline long lunch invitations (2 hours).

Before you can use transition time efficiently you need to eliminate the time-wasting ways in which you spend it now. What do you usually do when you have a few minutes to spare? Have a cup of coffee? Read the newspapers? Nothing at all?

See if you can eliminate some of the time-wasting moments. Can you do without your coffee? If you want to read the newspapers can you quickly mark the relevant articles for reading later? If you want to do nothing at all, can you go for a short walk to clear your head and give yourself a chance to think?

Reducing unproductive time gives you more time for doing things that really interest you or that are a useful part of your working day.

The art of doing two things at once

This is an important skill that turns transition or unproductive time into a useful part of your day. It is not impossible, home workers do it all the time. The typical home worker, whether doing paid work, community work or caring for a home and family, is adept at doing several things at once. Think what they have to do. In the morning, Angela puts on the kettle. While that is boiling she makes the toast. She gives the children their breakfast while she listens to the news on the radio.

A variation on this is combining tasks, that is doing them in the same space of time but not necessarily together. For example, Angela might drop off her library book on the same trip as taking the dry cleaning to town. This capability to see how many things can be combined into one piece of time not only saves time but makes you more efficient.

At work you can think in the same way. Listen to the news while dressing, or management tapes while driving. Take that report to your colleague when you are both at a meeting today, instead of making a separate trip tomorrow. Combine your weekly staff meeting with handing out minutes from a recent strategy meeting.

If you have to make a long train journey, plan to write some letters or read your documents. If you have to make a trip to another branch can you combine that with meeting someone whom you would otherwise have had to visit on another occasion. Make sure that every bit of your time is used to the full.

You want to be alone

You can use transition time best if you make time to be alone so you can concentrate for that short period of time. If you are likely to be interrupted in your office, why not see if the boardroom is empty and spend a quiet 20 minutes there. Or sit in an empty interview room.

If you cannot be alone and you are in a crowded place such as a waiting room or aeroplane, then create your own solitude 'shield'. For example, you can do this by wearing headphones and playing quiet music on the tape, by placing papers to signify that you do not want to be disturbed or by hiding behind a newspaper while you think. I'm sure you can think of other ways.

> ## *TIME MANAGEMENT TIP*
>
> Avoid making eye contact with people – this discourages them from stopping to chat.

Have a plan

If you have not planned what you can do in your spare time, then you will waste it. You should not find yourself with a slot of spare time and have nothing to do in it. If you want to make the best use of transition time you must prepare beforehand. A little planning will enable you to have what you need to hand whenever you have time to spare.

Think about what you can take with you to do at odd moments. Make a list of all the things you could do and then ensure that you have the relevant papers and other equipment in your case, or a special folder that is always ready to go with you.

The folder should always be up to date with reading material and notes, so that you do not have to waste time deciding what to do or be unable to work because you do not have the correct equipment.

> ## *TIME MANAGEMENT TIP*
>
> Ask your secretary to add routine reading matter to your folder, e.g. trade magazine, company newsletter.

Before you go out in the morning, or even the previous evening, prepare a few items for use in spare moments. Instead of taking a whole magazine with you, tear out the articles that interest you. Choose a book you've been meaning to read and mark the interesting chapters.

You don't want to fill your briefcase so that you can barely carry it, but make sure that you have a few essential things to hand. You will certainly have a pen and notebook and perhaps a dictating machine and a portable phone. Before you go anywhere put some of these items in your case so that you have something to do:

- articles torn from magazines that you would like to read
- a management book with important chapters marked
- a list of people to whom you owe letters/memos
- a document that needs proofreading
- a notebook for recording ideas/letters
- your diary/time planner
- some headed note paper, envelopes and compliment slips
- mobile phone
- laptop/notebook computer or electronic organiser.

You can pull out whichever piece of work most easily fits the situation and the time in hand. The notebook and paper is important because a dictating machine, although by far the most convenient and efficient method of dealing with correspondence, cannot always be used. Some situations, such as a waiting room, are not suitable for talking. The notebook and paper enable you to note the main points of your letter for your secretary to deal with later.

Quick correspondence tips

Headed note paper and envelopes enable you to write brief hand-written replies where appropriate. You can then pop them in an envelope, write on the address and they are ready for stamping. In the same way, a few compliment slips enable you to pass on material without having to return to the office to do so.

——— Seizing the moment ———

Much of your transition time will be obvious. You can anticipate the ten minutes between meetings, for example. But sometimes, you will find yourself with unexpected free time – perhaps a cancelled appointment or a delayed dinner date. It is now that your planning shows its worth. If you have prepared yourself with work as suggested earlier, then you should have something worthwhile to get on with. If you are in your office you might be able to get on with a major task if the time slot is long enough. Otherwise, take out your transitional folder and deal with the work in it. The more you get done, the less work will pile up during your main working hours.

Procrastination – the enemy of transition time

You cannot use the time effectively if you procrastinate. As soon as you are into transition time you must start working immediately or the time will disappear. I talk about overcoming procrastination in Chapter 5.

⸺ What to do in transition time ⸺

Transition time is not for dealing with the main work of the day that requires your full attention for long periods. It is, however, useful for those smaller tasks which often pile up until they take a disproportionate amount of your time, such as responding to letters or reading.

Your transition times might include longer periods of time that are difficult to deal with, such as travelling. But thanks to modern technology, even car travel can be productive. You could, for example, listen to a language tape while driving. (But be careful – if you find your attention wanders then stick to music.) Or on public transport, particularly trains, you can do paperwork or read. You can even use your portable phone to catch up on those calls you have to make. But again beware – you will not make yourself popular with other passengers if you do this. The sound of a carriage full of people using portable phones is off-putting for everyone and not conducive to concentration. Do as you would be done by.

Uses for transition time

All kinds of short projects can be fitted into transition time. You could do any of the following:

- make phone calls (particularly if you have a portable phone)
- write rough drafts of letters
- write office memos
- catch up on reading
- outline long- and short-term business plans
- make notes about new projects or systems
- note ideas arising from previous meetings, projects or conferences
- write next week's diary or management schedule
- deal with staff problems

- deal with routine work
- meet people
- think – ideas are important!
- listen to music
- listen to information tapes
- walk or do exercises to 'wake up'
- prepare questions for a meeting
- take a nap
- make appointments
- evaluate a previous meeting or appointment
- self-assessment.

What can you do in ten minutes?

Many time slots only last for short periods, perhaps ten or fifteen minutes. It might seem too much effort to do anything in such a short period. Here are some ideas of what you can do in a ten-minute slot that are useful and time saving:

- read a short article/report
- read some letters
- write/dictate a letter/memo
- proofread some pages
- prepare your diary/schedule for next week
- record ideas
- read/send e-mail
- write notes for a speech.

Reading takes time

A large part of many people's day revolves around reading material. Catching up with your reading makes good sense in transition time. But to make the most of it you need to be able to get to the relevant parts of any reading material quickly. There are tricks to reading quickly – I mention these in Chapter 7.

I am not going to advocate a speed-reading scheme. You can take one if you like but while it might improve your reading speed, not everyone wants to spend time practising it. But anyone can read articles, documents and books more quickly if they practise the following techniques:

1 Scan the chapter headings and index to see what is covered.
2 Read the book or article introduction and conclusion (most long documents will have a précis).
3 Read only the relevant chapters.
4 Read the chapter introduction and conclusion.
5 Read any important chapters more slowly, marking important points.
6 Articles – read the first few paragraphs to see if the rest is relevant, and the last two paragraphs. Only read the whole article if relevant.

By treating each piece of reading matter in this methodical way you can quickly learn to discard material that is of no use or interest, and to read the relevant pieces quickly.

You do not need to read every word of something unless it is important do so, for example when checking facts before publication. Forget the guilt you were made to feel at school if you didn't read every word of your story book. Nobody is going to tick you off if you only read three sentences. If those three sentences are all you need then that is all you need to read.

Match work to time quality

You will not be able to work on a long-term project during transition times but you can do routine and low grade work. Make sure that the kind of work you do during these 'dead' times matches the quality of the time. Travel time will warrant low grade or routine tasks. Short waiting periods can be used for quick tasks, half an hour before a conference dinner could be used for longer tasks requiring more concentration, and so on.

Do not try to do anything complicated or vitally important during transition time. Use it for getting routine but necessary tasks out of the way so that you can concentrate on high grade important tasks during your main working periods.

Time out is useful

Transition time can also be used to relax or take a little exercise. Don't dismiss transition time as a period for thinking and consolidating your thoughts. Sometimes the opportunity to sit quietly and muse is the best use of spare bits of time. It is not only relaxing but gives you a chance to consider problems of the day without interference. It needn't be long – just 20 minutes to sit quietly and think. Or take a brisk walk around the block to gather your thoughts. It can be invigorating and energising and gives you time to think as well as exercise.

A few minutes doing stretching exercises can relax you. In fact any kind of brief exercise will increase the adrenaline, relax you and clear your head. Alternatively, just sitting quietly with your eyes closed can be as beneficial, as can reading a chapter from a novel or doing a crossword. Not all your spare time can be spent like this but the odd moment makes the rest of the day bearable.

Mary, an accountant, makes a point of sitting quietly in her office for 20 minutes every day. Her secretary is given strict instructions to intercept all visitors or phone calls during that time. Those 20 minutes of reflection help Mary focus on her work overall.

Time-saving technology

Modern technology has transformed the use of transition time. It is now possible to conduct much of your work from out of the office.

Dictating machine

The dictating machine, so useful for recording letters and memos for your secretary to type up later, can also be used as a notebook for recording ideas.

Laptop computer

Laptop computers are very useful on trains, for example, and when staying in hotels. Where possible, plug them into the mains. Unfortunately the batteries on these machines do not last longer than a few hours and need recharging frequently.

Notebook computer/electronic organiser

The best tool is probably a notebook computer or the new multipurpose electronic organiser. Not only do they enable you to deal with your diary/schedule, they also have enough word-processing capacity to allow you to type a short article or memo. This can then be either directly printed out or transferred to your own or your secretary's computer at the office. Some are combined with a mobile phone. The smaller machines also have the added advantage of a longer battery life.

With both laptop computers and electronic organisers/notebook computers having the modern high-quality software e-mail, you will have all the advantages of the Internet. This makes it easy to read your e-mail, which can mount up considerably during the day, and to send replies. With a longer slot, perhaps half an hour between arrival and dinner at a hotel, you can search the Internet for information for a project.

Tape recorder

A tape recorder (not a dictating machine which uses small tapes) can be useful when travelling. A personal stereo or an in-car tape deck means that you can listen to recorded versions of management books, learn a language, reduce your stress, learn management techniques or even relax to music while you travel.

Extra work

Many business people use time at home or holidays for catching up on work. They come home from a hard day at the office and after a meal spend an hour or more on work. During the holidays they disappear to make calls or spend time on paperwork.

If you do this, you should rethink it. It is not only stressful, it is also unfair to your family. Even if you live alone, you need to have some time for leisure and relaxation, otherwise you will not perform at your best during working hours.

It is unrealistic nowadays to say that nobody should take work home with them. But when you next take work home, look through it carefully and decide whether you could have done it during the day or even not dealt with it at all. Make a note of what you could have done as you deal with each item and ask yourself the following questions:

- could someone else have dealt with this?
- did I need the whole of this document/article/book?
- could I have dealt with this during transition time?
- did this need to be dealt with at all?

You will probably find that at least half of the work you intended to do at home could have been dealt with during working hours.

If you must take work home, limit the time you spend on it. Allow yourself an hour, say, and then stop. Or limit yourself to three hours once a week. However you do it, do not allow it to take over your personal life.

Holiday time can be just as bad. Your loved ones will not appreciate it if you spend time in the hotel dealing with work rather than on the beach with them. Again, it is a question of limiting yourself. Sometimes you have to take work away with you. Derek, a senior manager, always has work to read during any holiday. He limits himself to one or two evenings towards the end of the holiday. By that time he has enjoyed the company of his family and had time to relax. He uses the last couple of evenings to ease himself back into working mode.

If you find you are constantly overloaded with work to take home, then use this book to rethink your working day. Give careful consideration to whether you are delegating enough work to others. The name of the game nowadays is empowerment. Successful people allow their staff to take on responsibility as far as their ability allows. This gives their staff a sense of purpose and frees them for more important work (see Chapter 10 on the art of delegating).

Pay for time

If you or your company can afford it, do not feel guilty about paying for someone to deal with routine jobs that need to be done but which take up an unnecessarily large part of your time or that of your staff. For example, at home you might pay someone to do the ironing or clean the house. At work you might employ somebody to stuff envelopes or deliver documents. Whatever it is, the cost will be justified by saving your more valuable time for more important work.

TIME MANAGEMENT TIP

Be prepared to pay for quality and reliability – it is still cheaper than 'employing' yourself to do the job.

TOP TEN TIPS

1 Identify your transition times or 'dead' times.
2 Have a plan for transition times.
3 Keep a folder of work ready.
4 Do two things at once whenever possible.
5 Don't make two journeys when one will do.
6 When you have some spare time put it to use at once.
7 Match the quality of work to the time you have spare.
8 Keep a few minutes for relaxation.
9 Use time-saving technology whenever possible and appropriate.
10 Don't take work home if you can avoid it.

Summary

Transition time or 'dead' time is the wasted pockets of time during our day. It also includes preparatory time that could be reduced or used more productively. This time can be used constructively. Identify your transition times and list what you can do in them. Reduce wasteful time and try to do two things at once whenever possible. Find a quiet place to concentrate or create your own solitude 'shield'. Have a specific plan for how you will use transition time. Keep a special folder for transition time work and take it with you whenever you leave the office. Don't forget to use some transition time for thinking and relaxation.

5
CONQUER PROCRASTINATION

This chapter tells you how to get started when you don't want to. It explains what procrastination is, why you procrastinate and how to deal with it. It gives practical tips for beating that 'don't want to start' feeling.

If you don't start you can't finish

Procrastination is the art of putting off doing something. We can all find something better to do than the job in hand. That extra cup of coffee, reading the papers, watching TV, clarifying the project just once more with your boss, are all procrastination techniques. But those letters sitting in your in-tray need to be dealt with *now*.

The problem with procrastinating is that the work still has to be done and if you put it off eventually you find yourself trying to cram it all into a short time. This will make you even more frustrated. When it comes down to it, the only way to get things done is to start doing them.

It is easy to let procrastination become a habit rather than a once-in-a-while thing. Why do we put off doing things? Common reasons include:

- fear of failure
- boredom with the task
- other things are more interesting
- lack of time

- you're scared of it
- you don't know how to do it
- you are setting yourself a very high standard
- you're trying to do too much
- you're tired
- you don't believe it's worth doing
- you haven't defined your goals
- you've got other problems that are worrying you.

The list could go on and on and your reasons for not getting on with the job will be different from mine.

Some of the reasons for not starting a task have things in common. Fear of failure and setting yourself a high standard have the common theme of feeling that you are not good enough to do the task well. Being scared of it, not knowing how to do it or being unsure of your goals mean that you are unsure of how to tackle the work. Lack of time and trying to do too much show a lack of organisational skills. If you are bored with the task itself or think it not worthwhile or have other things that you would rather be doing, then you need to rethink your attitude to the job. If you are tired or concerned with other problems, then these are practical problems that can be resolved.

Catherine, the manager of a small printing company, is a typical procrastinator. The sheer volume of her work seems insurmountable and makes her put off tackling it. She often finds herself working late because she has put off so many tasks during the day. The amount of paperwork on her desk overwhelms her and it takes a lot of cups of coffee and chats with her staff before she gets down to the work on her desk. This is frustrating for her staff because they have to keep chasing her for instructions and paperwork. It is tiring and depressing for Catherine because she feels trapped by it all.

Fortunately for you and Catherine, and however and why ever you procrastinate, the ways to deal with it are similar. You need to do a number of things:

- start *now*
- define exactly what needs to be done
- divide the cake – tackle the job in small steps
- prioritise the tasks to be done
- decide on the deadline
- eliminate interruptions

- do the first task *now*
- leave time for corrections, review and collation.

Start now

Whatever the job that you have to do there is only one way to get to grips with it – start *now*. You cannot plunge headfirst into whatever tasks you need to do to complete the job unless you know what they are and how they should be done. But you can start *now* on the preparation stage of gathering information and materials and deciding how the job should be tackled. By getting to grips straight away with sorting out the problem you are already well on the way to getting to the end.

TIME MANAGEMENT TIP

Give yourself a deadline for getting the preparations completed. You then have no excuse for delaying the start of the first task.

— What do you really have to do? —

First look at your work and decide what really has to be done. If you are in charge of producing a report, you will have to gather the information, consult colleagues, write the report, ask colleagues for comments, get the report typed up and then collated into a suitable format. Depending on the status of the report this might mean organising special printing, covers and binding.

So what exactly is *your* job? Your secretary or assistant can be sent to gather certain kinds of information if they are given guidelines and a deadline. Your colleagues can comment on the draft typescript if given a deadline. The printing can be organised by your secretary/assistant. You will define the wording on the cover and approve the design but the rest can be left to the experts – either in-company or outside. Finally, you will check and approve the cover, for example, before bulk production. Your secretary can organise distribution to people on your list.

So what seems to be a large task leaves you with only certain things to do:

- decide the deadlines for each part of the work
- collate the information
- write the report (this can be done in shorter stages)
- incorporate colleagues' comments
- approve wording and design of the cover
- check the final draft and design
- compile list of recipients
- check and approve final proofs.

Dividing the cake – taking small steps

You would not eat a whole cake in one sitting all by yourself (at least I hope you wouldn't!). You would naturally slice it up and devour each slice one at a time until it was gone. The same principle applies to any task that you have to tackle. And this is a way of making it seem less daunting. It is much easier to get started on a small piece of anything than tackle the whole thing in one go. Catherine, for example, looked at the work she had to do each day and envisaged it as one long task that she had no chance of completing. No wonder she was too scared to get started until late in the day.

Once you have worked out exactly what you need to do, you can divide each of the tasks necessary to complete a job into smaller steps. So, for checking the final draft and design, for example, you would:

- timetable a period for making the checks
- ensure that the originals are to hand
- proofread the words
- check the design elements against specification and design
- mark any final amendments to be made
- arrange for copy to be sent to the printer with final instructions.

This method can be applied to anything you have to do. Make each step small enough that you feel happy tackling it. Then go on to the next one. By doing it bit by bit you will get it all done.

This is only an example of how any task that seems overwhelming can be reduced to manageable proportions. Each separate part can then be divided into further sections. For example, when compiling a report, you might spend part of a morning writing the introduction and two afternoons writing the main body of it.

Prioritise your tasks

If a job seems overwhelming it could be because you don't know where to start. If you simply start with the first task to hand and work through, it will seem endless and you will get depressed with it. You will use that as an excuse to delay. You cannot hope to tackle anything successfully unless you know in which order you are going to complete each step.

As with any task, work out what steps it can be divided into and then prioritise them. Do those that need the most research or organisation first, and then the others. Alternatively, start with the easiest task to give you inspiration and then tackle a more difficult one once you are in the mood. You will find that once you have begun working on the task, it will seem easier and less daunting.

TIME MANAGEMENT TIP

Set an alarm to go off five minutes after you sit down at your desk. When it goes, start work straight away.

Set deadlines

In order to get things done you need to set deadlines. Sometimes these will be imposed by other people – particular tasks will be already built into your day, week, month or year, for example, the conference speech that has to be written by the beginning of March; you have two days to write up the minutes of the chairman's meeting; the cake for the jumble sale has to be at the village hall by Saturday morning.

If you have not been given deadlines, set your own. If you want to write that novel, decide to complete it in one year; give yourself from January until the beginning of July to learn basic Spanish; allow yourself two weeks to produce that proposal for your line manager; give yourself half an hour to answer your morning post.

Deadlines are not as awful as you might think. Instead of treating them as a terrible thing that sends you into a panic, look on them as a helpful tool to aid your organisation. With all deadlines, whether imposed or self-determined, work back from them. When you divide your task up into smaller steps, decide how long you can spend on each step and where you can fit it into your schedule. Allow yourself ample time at the end for checking and making any final additions or alterations. This last point is important. Research students, for example, often underestimate the time needed to check and write up their bibliography and list of footnotes.

TIME MANAGEMENT TIP

If, once you've started, you get into the flow of the task and don't want to stop, ignore the deadline!

If the task still seems daunting, combine deadlines for each step and the task as a whole with rewards. For example, when I have finished writing a chapter of a book I allow myself half an hour reading a novel. If you are working in an office, for example, save your rewards up. Have a 'reward list' and save your reward until the end of the day or the weekend.

Reward yourself

There is no harm in bribing yourself to complete a piece of work. Promise yourself a reward for each part of a project or major task that you complete. It might be something as simple as a bar of chocolate or another cup of coffee, but if it works for you, do it.

Make appointments with yourself

You can help beat procrastination by making dates with yourself to start and complete tasks. Instead of dealing with it when it occurs to you or putting it off until the last minute, timetable tasks into your diary. You then have no excuse for doing something else because your time has been allocated for that task. This works for small tasks as well as the steps for completing longer projects. Tell yourself that you have made a date to do the work and start on time.

Eliminate interruptions

Dealing with interruptions is a great excuse for procrastinators. Phone calls, visitors, salespeople, people just 'dropping in' all provide an opportunity for delaying tactics. In order to defeat your inclination to procrastinate you need to eliminate as many interruptions as possible.

Dealing with phone calls is dealt with in detail in Chapter 8. Suffice it to say that using an answering machine or arranging for your secretary to answer the phone for you at certain times will free you from many interruptions by telephone.

Visitors are more difficult to deal with. If your section is expected to deal with visitors, arrange for a member of staff to have responsibility for them at certain times or on certain days, so that you are free to get on with your work. You could delegate staff to be responsible for visitors for one day a week each on a rota basis, so that everyone gets a chance to work uninterrupted.

Salespeople could simply be told by your secretary that they will only be seen on certain days at certain times. Alternatively, delegate a member of staff to deal with them. Normally they should not get further than the main entrance or a phone call to your secretary.

The most difficult people to deal with are those who pass your office (or desk in an open-plan office) and pop over 'just for a chat' or 'because its quicker than phoning' or they 'knew you'd be in'. They often start with the assertion that the visit will be 'just for ten minutes' but they often last much longer – especially if you use it as an excuse not to get down to work. These interruptions not only waste time but give you an excellent excuse for not getting on with your work.

You need to have a strategy for dealing with casual callers. First, decide who you will stop work for. Your boss would presumably come into this category, but even then if you need to get on with work you could ask if you could get back to them later when you've finished it. Otherwise, decide how to keep casual visitors from your door. This is particularly important if your office is not in a situation that can be guarded by your secretary or staff. If you are 'guarded', casual visitors can be intercepted unless they are in a 'permitted' category.

You do not necessarily want to deter all contact and many managers like to operate an 'open door' policy. But too many casual visitors can result in little actual work getting done, with the excuse that 'people interaction' is more important. You need to use strategies that make you accessible, but on your terms.

Reduce personal interruptions by trying these tactics:

- put a notice on your door or desk showing when you are available (red for 'keep out', green for 'free', perhaps)
- make it clear you are not available to visitors between certain hours or on certain days
- go and work somewhere else, for example an interview room, the board room, the library
- shut your door.

TIME MANAGEMENT TIP

If your desk faces the door, don't look up every time someone passes, otherwise it will encourage them to stop and chat. If possible, move your desk so that it faces away from the door or the main flow of people.

Do it now

When you have worked out what to do, decide which is the first task and *do it now*. Whatever you feel about a particular task, the best way of dealing with it is to start on it as soon as possible, not to put it off. Making even a small inroad into it will improve your reaction towards it and make it easier to continue. It helps to have divided your task into smaller sections, as recommended previously.

If you still find it hard to get started, try these tips:

- do the easiest part first to encourage yourself, or
- do the hardest part first so the rest will seem easier
- make sure everything is ready for you to start straight away
- if you must have that cup of coffee, take it to your desk with you
- promise yourself a reward for each part completed, such as reading a few pages of a favourite book, a short walk in the fresh air, a sweet
- visualise the successful completion of the task
- start anywhere and do anything just to get started (writers stuck for inspiration often write down whatever comes into their head onto a blank sheet of paper just to get started).

Leave time for corrections, review and collation

The worst result of procrastination is that you do not leave yourself enough time to do all the things that have to be done to finish a job. These include checking the result and making any corrections that are necessary. You must also allow time to review the result and decide whether it is what you hoped to achieve or whether there was any other way that you could have done it that might have been better, quicker or cheaper. Finally, you need to ensure that all parts of the job are complete and to gather them together to be put in the final form. Another brief check of the complete project and you are finished.

If you don't allow yourself enough time for doing this you will end up falling behind and panicking. If you know that you have allowed yourself enough time you will be happier about getting on with the job.

When you are estimating how long to allow for this review time, use a previous similar job as an example and timetable the length of time required accordingly. Allow a bit of spare time for extras and you should have no problem in completing the tasks well within your deadline. Knowing that you will not have a panic at the last minute will give you the confidence to get started.

TIME MANAGEMENT TIP

Allow yourself only one revision or one reassessment and correction of any work or task.

Good enough is good enough

You might be one of those people who puts things off because you are afraid that the end result will be less than perfect. You set yourself high standards and become afraid of not living up to your own expectations.

You are making the mistake of assuming that others have equally high expectations of you. Yes, they want the job done well and on time to a standard suitable for the job. But if you continually put work off because you are afraid of presenting less than your own best standard, you risk turning in work late and irritating your boss and colleagues.

The work you need to produce needs to be good enough for the job – no more and no less. If you have done the work, checked it, made sure it is a suitable standard for the task and it is as good as you can manage in the time, do not do any more. Obsessively checking everything again and again won't improve it; the more you do that the more frightened you will be of completing it, let alone starting it.

———— Get it right first time ————

Aim to complete the work correctly the first time. Obviously, you will not always manage this and a final check is sensible, but at least try. Not only does it make each task a personal challenge, thus making even dull tasks more interesting, but it speeds the whole process up.

You can improve your chances of doing things right by preparing beforehand. Make sure that you have allowed yourself enough time to tackle the part of the job that you are going to do. Read through any information and instructions beforehand. Gather together all the information, components and tools to do the job properly. Arrange these in the best order to complete the work. Make enough notes to guide you. Start now.

Try to work steadily through the steps needed to complete the task. At the same time try to complete each piece of work to the highest standard you can. This will not eliminate the need for a revision or check afterwards but should reduce the amount of corrective work to be done.

You might think that this means you will work much slower because you will be continually correcting work as you go along. That will not be the case. You will work steadily rather than in fits and starts, and because you have done the preparation carefully you should have less need to correct as you go.

Some companies are so keen on the idea of 'right first time' that they make it the aim of every part of their production or work process.

What happens when you're not perfect?

None of us is perfect. You can do the best you can at any task and still not get it right. Sometimes this will not be your fault. Peter, for example, following the guidelines above, regularly produces satisfactory statistical analyses for his boss at the insurance company where he works. But his last piece of work was sent back to be redone. This was because the company had decided to use different criteria for some sections so that in spite of accurate work on his part, Peter's analyses were incorrect.

On other occasions, you may have made mistakes or not produced your best work. We all have our off days. Don't let it get you down. Accept that you have made a mistake. Find out exactly where you went wrong (ask if you need to) and then tackle that part again, having checked your preparation. As long as most of it is right, any reworking of a task should not take too long.

Think positively

To get work done you need to have a positive attitude to it. If you approach any task with the attitude that you don't want to do it, or you think it is boring or you hate it, you will not do it well and it will take a lot longer to do. You will constantly be thinking of ways not to do it rather than getting on with it.

Having a positive attitude can affect all aspects of your work. Angela, one of a pool of secretaries to middle managers in a large retail company, considered her job boring and disliked the environment she worked in. Her work was satisfactory but she always handed it in just before any deadline because she kept putting it off. Her bosses found her attitude irritating and disliked having to phone her constantly to make sure the work reached them in time.

A friend pointed out to Angela that her attitude was doing her no favours – her chances of promotion were slim and her colleagues disliked her moaning. Angela took a look at the way she worked and decided to change it. She tidied up her work space and added personal touches to inspire her. She tried to react to each piece of work she was given as if it was a new and exciting project, treating each job as a personal challenge. Even with the most mundane of tasks she set herself a deadline, envisaged a positive outcome and tried to complete it to the highest standard she could. Her work was presented earlier and her general attitude became more positive. She even started to volunteer to complete extra tasks because she had made time by reorganising her way of working. Angela's colleagues found her easier to get on with, and she found that she was beginning to enjoy her work more because she approached it positively and her bosses, noticing the changes, began to consider her for a PA job.

This is an extreme example, of course, but the same thing applies to you. If you take a positive attitude to even the most unwelcome or unpleasant of tasks then you will reap the benefits. Not least of these will be the completion of the task in good time and to an acceptable standard. Do not underestimate the satisfaction of work well done.

——————— Don't be late ———————

One common result of procrastination is that you will be late for appointments. It is tempting to put off unpopular appointments such as meeting with an unpleasant client or your child's head teacher until the last moment. You arrive anything from a few minutes to half an hour late and apologise. But the meeting has got off on the wrong foot. Nobody likes waiting for someone to arrive for a prearranged time. Some people may forgive; others will simply dismiss you. Not only is it the height of discourtesy, it also wastes their time – and yours. Not everyone will wait for you or still keep the appointment. It is particularly difficult if other people are waiting to be seen and most people have other things to do. Fitting you in is normally a courtesy.

Lateness can have serious consequences. Arnold, a solicitor, arrived late for a lunch appointment with a new, potentially rewarding client. He was only ten minutes late but by then the client had gone. He later discovered that the client had said 'Why should I pay good money to a company whose staff don't take my time seriously?' By not bothering to turn up on time, a lucrative account had been lost. Nobody likes people who think them so unimportant that they keep them waiting.

You can be on time

If you are someone who wants to get to places on time but always seems to get there late, then it is time to change your ways. You are probably simply disorganised. You may also be one of those few people who do not wear a watch. If so, you should reconsider. If you cannot wear a wrist watch, then consider an alternative – an elegant fob watch, a pretty version of a nurse's watch, a watch on a pendant, keeping a watch in your pocket. Put wall clocks in your bedroom, kitchen/breakfast room and office. If you use an electronic organiser, always set the alarm to sound before your next appointment – but remember to allow sufficient time to get there easily.

If you are normally chronically late then take action. Let's start with getting out of the house on time. Here are some guidelines:

- buy an alarm clock for your home and use it. Choose one that sounds loud and long enough to wake you up. Position it away from your bed so you have to get up to switch it off
- arrange for a phone 'wake-up call'. Ask your telephone operator how to do this
- set your clocks/watch/alarms five minutes early
- choose and arrange your clothes the night before
- layout your breakfast requirements the night before
- have your briefcase/handbag already packed
- make sure your keys and wallet/purse are always in the same place.

The above tips will get you out of bed, into the shower, breakfasted and out of your door on time. But how can you get to your appointments in general on time during the day?

First of all, use everyone you can to help you. Tell your secretary to remind you in plenty of time when you have to leave. Depending on the circumstances, ask the other person's secretary or a friend to give you a call to remind you. Arrange for transport such as a taxi or company car so that you have to be ready on time.

Rearranging time to avoid lateness

An effective way of reducing the times you are late is to look carefully at your schedules and diary and eliminate or reduce occasions when you cannot get to places on time. Look at the time you have allowed yourself to get from your office to a meeting with clients in a nearby town, for example. Have you left enough time? Do you know how you are getting there? If you are travelling by public transport, have you checked the timetable? Are you travelling by the most direct route?

Always allow yourself extra time for getting places. Arriving early is no crime and is usually admirable. Arriving late universally is not. If you do arrive early you can always use the time usefully (see Chapter 4).

For internal appointments rearrange your schedule if you only have a few minutes to get from office A to office B on the other side of the building. Where possible, change tight schedules to allow yourself enough time to get there comfortably and ensure that you set your alarm to remind you to start out early.

Know the route

Don't rely on your memory or guesswork to discover how to get to your destination. Work out your route beforehand and be clear how you will be getting there. Perhaps try one of the new in-car route finders or use a route finder computer program on your PC beforehand. If you are going by car make sure that it is in working order the day before. Consult road organisations for up-to-date traffic conditions; use your car radio to get up-to-the-minute local traffic information.

Use this information sensibly. The most direct route may not be the quickest if it is usually blocked with traffic. Some routes become blocked at certain times of the day or week. See if you can reschedule your appointment to take account of this.

If using public transport, find out the most direct route and check the departure and arrival times to allow yourself time to get from the station or depot to your appointment. If possible, buy (or get your secretary to organise) tickets beforehand to save time. This not only saves you from the risk of missing your transport by queuing for tickets, but is usually cheaper. Reserved seats can be booked on a train beforehand and this will save you from searching carriages for an unoccupied seat during busy times.

Allow for the worst

If you are often late, make sure that you are allowing enough time for the unexpected. If you miss the bus, for example, have you allowed enough time to walk? Have you got enough money for a taxi?

Always allow for the worst to happen – if it doesn't you'll be early. If it does, you still have a good chance of getting there on time.

Phone ahead

Always have the phone number of the place you are going to so that you can phone if it seems you will be unavoidably detained. Carry a mobile phone so that you don't have to waste time searching for a public phone. Phoning ahead if you are delayed enables the other person to rearrange your appointment, or allows them do something else while waiting for you. It is courteous to let them know of the delay and convinces them that you are taking their time seriously.

Leave early

This might seem rude if you have taken the trouble to get to an appointment on time. However, most meetings continue after they need to. By indicating on arrival that you have to leave at a certain time, you ensure that business is dealt with straight away and you can leave with a clear conscience. Even allowing an extra ten minutes, by leaving ten minutes early, you can reach your next appointment on time. Meetings can be run more efficiently and effectively too. See Chapter 9 for advice on how to reduce the time meetings take and run them more efficiently.

TOP TEN TIPS

1 Do it now.
2 Know exactly what you need to do.
3 Prioritise your tasks.
4 Divide tasks into smaller steps.
5 Decide deadlines.
6 Eliminate interruptions.
7 Allow time for checking.
8 Don't try to be perfect.
9 Don't be late.
10 Allow for delays.

Summary

Procrastination can be caused by fear, boredom, worry or many other things. The most important rule for beating procrastination is to start *now*. Divide any large task into smaller steps. Prioritise each task and set deadlines for completion. Do your best – most work needs to be good enough, not perfect. Try to do any task correctly the first time you do it. Think positively about each task and visualise its completion. Devise strategies to stop yourself being late. Timetable even simple tasks so that you make a definite date with yourself to do them. Don't be afraid to bribe yourself to complete a task.

6

LEARN TO SAY 'NO'

This chapter explains why saying no is a time management tool and how to use it effectively. It explains why some people can't say no and provides techniques for saying no politely but firmly.

The secret of saying 'no'

Saying no is one of the best-kept secrets of time management. Even if you carry out all the suggestions in this book, if you don't learn to say no your efforts will be wasted.

Think of all the times that you have agreed to do things you didn't really want to do. At the time it probably seemed easier to say yes. You probably felt that you couldn't refuse. To do so would have made you feel guilty; or perhaps you simply couldn't think of a good excuse. You then found yourself doing something that took up your time, didn't contribute to your own priorities, and that you didn't want to do. But are there good reasons for not saying yes?

Why saying 'yes' wastes time

If you find it hard to say no to requests and agree to most things asked of you, you are wasting time. Not only are you committed to doing something for others instead of getting on with your own priorities, you will also feel anxious, depressed and resentful.

Doing too much for others means that there is less time for your own work. It piles up and you overwork and become prone to stress and anxiety. Many things you agree to do for others will be non-essential according to your own priorities and you will feel trapped and annoyed.

Tanya, a sales clerk, was always being given extra work to do by her boss. Her colleagues often asked to her do work for them 'to help out'. She tried to be helpful and do it all by putting her own work second. She found that she never seemed to get to her main work until the end of the week and began to feel angry and put upon. Because she thought she did not have the right to refuse, she kept her feelings to herself. One exceptionally busy day when a colleague asked her to deal with yet another piece of work, she finally snapped and yelled at him. When her boss found out, she was horrified. 'If only you'd said something. We thought you were keen to take on the extra work.'

Tanya's story has a happy ending. She and her colleagues have come to an agreement about what they can and cannot take on for others. Her boss has agreed a sensible workload. But the warning is for all of us. It doesn't pay to say yes all the time.

Most people have been brought up to be polite to others. It is therefore a natural reaction to want to please others and to make life easy for everyone by agreeing wherever possible. However, this does not help you manage your time properly; nor does saying yes to everything necessarily endear you to others. They may take you for granted when anything needs to be done and show less respect for you. They are less likely to respect your own need for getting on with your own work.

——— Saving time by saying 'no' ———

How will saying no save you time? First of all, it will free you from non-essential tasks – all those things that you do to please other people but that are not essential to your own life. They can add up to a great deal of your time being spent on other people's priorities.

You should be doing things that contribute to your own goals and objectives first; other people's aims should be included only when you have the time, energy and inclination. Obviously you won't want to refuse to do something for your friends or your boss and colleagues. But neither will you want be put in a position where your own considerations have to take a back seat.

Next, you will save time by not accepting work that will interfere with your own or that will give it a lower priority. If your boss asks you to do the occasional piece of overtime or an extra piece of work, that's fine. If you are always being asked to do extra and it is not really relevant or useful to your own work, then it is not fine.

Finally, you will save time by saying no because you will not need to cope with the guilt and stress that agreeing to everything can induce. Worrying about not letting people down or how you can fit in extra things is in itself a time-waster. So is becoming ill because of the strain.

Saying no frees you to concentrate on things that are important to you.

TIME MANAGEMENT TIP

Eliminate interruptions. By doing so you give people less chance to ask you to do things.

———————— When to say 'no' ————————

It may not always be obvious when to say no to something. Should you say no to your colleague's request for help with a project when you are busy with your own work? Do you refuse to give a friend's child a lift to school when you will have to go out of your way to do so and it will make you late for work?

Be clear in your own mind what you want out of life and what your priorities are. The first chapters in this book will have helped you decide these. The things that you agree to do should contribute in some way to these goals. That does not mean you should be selfish and refuse to do anything for other people, but, if doing something will seriously undermine your time and energy and not contribute to your main priorities, then you should refuse.

For example, if you are always asked to take minutes for meetings that are nothing to do with your own work, you should say no. If you are continually asked to stay late at the office even though your private life suffers, you should say no. If doing extra work for your boss prevents you from doing the work the company is paying you for, you should say no.

Don't feel guilty

Many people have an inbuilt guilt barometer which makes them feel bad when refusing anything to anybody. Perhaps they were brought up to be polite to everyone and find it hard to refuse because it seems rude. Or perhaps they want to please people because they think it will make them more likeable. Or maybe they just don't know how to say no. Do you recognise yourself in any of these examples? If so, stop feeling guilty now. You have every right to refuse to do something you don't want to do. You can be sure that most people will do so without a second thought. Think of the successful and most confident people you know. Can you imagine them saying yes to everything and everyone? Of course not.

Don't get defensive or start giving excuses. You are within your rights to refuse. If you can't think of a good reason for saying no, keep quiet and don't say anything. People often say yes just to fill in a silence.

———— How to say 'no' ————

That's all very well, you might say, but how do I say no without seeming rude or aggressive? Is there a better way than just saying no bleakly?

The important thing to remember is that however you refuse the work, the word no should come first in the sentence. Unless it does the person you are speaking to will take it as a chink in your determination and assume that you can be talked round. However, if saying no on its own is too direct for you, temper it by providing a polite addition to the sentence. So, an example of refusing politely might be:

- no, I'm sorry but I can't help with the sale on Saturday
- no, I'm afraid I've got to finish this report
- no, we've already arranged to go out that evening
- no, I can't come round now.

If you are only refusing for that particular occasion you could add a modifying sentence such as:

- ... but I can help out next month
- ... but can we arrange to meet next week instead?

- ... but would you and Betty like to come to dinner on the 21st?
- ... but if it's urgent Sam might have time to do some of it (let Sam find his own excuse!).

An effective way of refusing is to acknowledge what the other person has said and then say why you can't do it. This shows that you realise the person has a genuine reason for asking for your help and so makes the refusal more acceptable. So, for example, you might say, 'You've obviously got a lot of work to do on that report, Sandra. But, no, I'm afraid my time is all spoken for.'

Assertion not aggression

You want to say no but you don't want to sound rude. You want to be firm but you don't want to sound aggressive. How can you do it?

Refusing to do something does not mean that you have to say so loudly and fiercely. But it might come out like that if you are not used to saying no. This is probably because you are nervous. After all, if you have been saying yes to everyone all your life, saying no takes a lot of courage. It may also be due to the fact that people are surprised at the new confident you and react differently. This makes you react more fiercely that you intended.

Don't be put off. Practise saying no at home in front of the mirror and into a tape recorder. Try to keep your voice firm but at a normal level. Speak clearly but confidently. This applies to all kinds of speaking. Make sure that you know why you are refusing so that you don't sound nervous.

If you are angry or annoyed with the other person you are in danger of refusing abruptly and rudely. Try the old trick of counting to ten before you say anything. This will calm you down and give you time to frame a suitably polite refusal.

The 'broken record' trick

Most people will accept your refusal with good grace and think none the worse of you for it. In fact they will probably respect you for having the courage to do what you know is right. But some people cannot accept refusals. They take it as a personal challenge to try and get you to change your mind. In that case you will have to resort to becoming a broken record. You do so by simply repeating no and your reasons in as many different ways as are necessary. Always starting with the word no, of course. In time, after hearing your refusal again and again, even the most persistent person will give in.

So you could be saying:

- no, I can't meet you on Tuesday
- no, I'm sorry but Tuesday's out of the question
- no, I'm afraid I'm busy on Tuesday
- no, Tuesday's impossible for me
- no, I've got no free time at all on Tuesday
- no, etc...

Say it with a smile

Most people can forgive a refusal if it is said in a pleasant manner and with a smile. A smile tells the person you are speaking to that you still like them. Your refusal is then accepted with good grace. Curiously, this works on the phone too. You might not think that a smile can be conveyed down a phone line but it can. People can pick up nuances of speech and tone of voice even at a distance. So your refusal with a smile over the phone will sound just that.

Say what you mean

Don't say maybe if you mean no otherwise the person you are speaking to will take this to mean that you are genuinely considering accepting. If you mean to refuse, do so. On the other hand, you may really need time to think about it. If so, ask for time to consider or consult your diary. But only do so if you really think that you might be able or want to do it.

If you need more information before you can make your mind up, ask for it straight away. Then you can decide quickly whether to refuse or accept.

When you give a reason for refusing, use a real reason such as 'I haven't got any free time this month' rather than 'it's not my kind of thing'. Real reasons are acceptable; feeble excuses sound like what they are. If you just don't want to do it be honest and say 'I'm sorry, but it's not something I'd ever feel like doing'.

Don't make someone else an excuse for refusing. You can't nowadays say 'my partner won't let me' without sounding feeble. Saying 'I can't because ...' emphasises that it is your own decision based on your own priorities that deserve respect.

In all cases of refusal make the no firm but leave the listener with the impression that you are still pleased to have heard from them. No on its own is usually too bleak but the formulae suggested are acceptable and more open. Use no on its own for persistent, insensitive people or troublemakers.

Don't forget to say 'thank you'

On many occasions you will not be asked to do something but will be offered something that the other person thinks might please you, perhaps a different job, a trip to the theatre or the chance to go canoeing. On these occasions, if you want to refuse, your first words should be thank you. 'Thank you, that's a lovely idea, but I ...' is an acceptable formula. After all, the other person thinks they are doing you a favour and you want to make it clear that you appreciate the offer and leave the way open to further communication.

TIME MANAGEMENT TIP

Trust your instincts – if you immediately think 'no' you are probably right.

—— How to say 'no' to your boss ——

Saying no to your boss or colleagues at work must be one of the hardest things to do. You are working for and with them and they expect you to be willing to contribute in any way that will help the company prosper. But this should not be to the extent of taking on too much extra work that leaves you resentful and exhausted and unable to complete your main work.

Obviously, depending on the job, a certain amount of give and take is required. In an emergency everybody is expected to help. But if you are constantly being asked to do extra or to do things that you do not agree with, what can you do?

First, be clear about the amount of work you are expected to do. If you are constantly being asked to do extra work, arrange to talk to your boss about it. Together you should agree an acceptable workload for you – an agreed general workload and negotiated overtime work. Evaluate jobs together and ask your boss how long each job should take. Work out how much time you have to spare. You and your boss can then agree the workload and timetable bearing in mind your present commitments.

You and your boss should agree:

- your job description
- normal workload
- acceptable overtime
- deadlines
- amount of notice needed for extra work
- timetable for major projects.

You should be clear about other commitments that make certain overtime work impossible. At the same time be prepared to agree to reasonable extra demands. You should both be clear about what is acceptable. Once this has been done you can then refuse extra work with a clear conscience – 'No, I'm sorry, you know I have that report to finish.'

If you are asked to do extra work on top of that already agreed and you think it is justified and that you can fit it in, negotiate separately about how much of it you can do and by when. Don't agree to take on extra work just for the sake of being seen to be on the boss's side. Any boss worth working for will not want employees who are working beyond their capacity.

You might not want to refuse because you are afraid of jeopardising your career or think that other people will be unwilling to help you on different occasions. But your career will depend on doing the work you have to do well, not on taking everything on and doing much of it badly under stress.

If you are worried about this, explain clearly why you have to refuse. 'No, I'm sorry I can't do that report now. I have four urgent pieces of work to finish' or 'No, I'm afraid I can't work overtime tonight. I already have another commitment', or even 'No, I don't agree with that. It would be wrong to add my comments to it.'

You don't want to seem to be obstructive so don't automatically refuse everything that comes your way. If your boss asks you to do something, sound positive but ask for time to see how it fits in with your other commitments. If you can fit the work in, fine. Otherwise write a memo detailing your commitments and the time you have available. Include a recommendation for how you could deal with the new work. For example, you could suggest cutting back on other work, doing a job for a limited period of time or enlisting the help of other staff. Your boss can then see that you have good reasons for refusing and will either accept proposals for reducing your workload to enable you to take on the extra work or will assign it to somebody else.

Don't be afraid of saying no at work. You are entitled to be respected for the work you do and to hold an opinion on it. You are also entitled to be understood to be the best person to know how much work you can sensibly take on.

—— Say 'no' to your colleagues ——

If your colleagues constantly ask you to do extra work you should be asking yourself why they are not coping with what they have got. It might be time to ask management to implement a time management seminar for everybody. (There is more about time management training in Chapter 12.) Meanwhile, the same responses apply. Accept extra work when you feel you can reasonably fit it in and you think it would be genuinely useful to do so, or that it will further your own priorities. If it will be too time consuming or otherwise unhelpful then do not do it. Give reasons and stick to them.

Some give and take is required in any job so you won't want to refuse everything but most of the time you should be concentrating on your own work and priorities. Body signals and language are important here. Do not sound apologetic or look embarrassed. Refuse politely but firmly. Roger, a secondary school teacher, was always being asked to take extra classes or attend out-of-school meetings not relevant to his subject. He had less and less time for preparing his own lessons or for working with his upper-sixth pupils' 'after school' club. His attempts to refuse were weak and he felt embarrassed saying no. One day he collapsed outside his classroom, was diagnosed with stress and spent four months off sick. During that time he re-evaluated his priorities. Now he politely and firmly refuses any extra work unless he can see that it is absolutely necessary to the school. He is more relaxed in the classroom because he has his own work under control and has time to help his sixth formers outside of school hours. His advice is, 'Colleagues don't respect you if you seem to be a pushover. You are more use at work if you are working well at the job you are paid to do. By all means help out – but only when really necessary, not out of habit or guilt.'

Saying 'no' to friends

Saying no to friends can be even more difficult because you have a more intimate relationship with them. You might be afraid that if you refuse them you will not hear from them again or that they will say nasty things about you behind your back. Or you might simply want to please them because you like them and feel that that is what friends are for.

If your friends are the kind who will think less of you for refusing something, are you sure that you want to know them? A true friend will simply accept that sometimes you can say yes and that other times you cannot. Do not feel, either, that you should be agreeing to everything your friend suggests. You would be a boring person if you did not have other calls on your time. Do not feel guilty about refusing. You can add a reason to your refusal and arrange to help them or see them on another occasion. This is part of the give and take of life.

TIME MANAGEMENT TIP

Write 'NO' on a piece of card and pin it where you can see it. This will remind you not to say 'yes' automatically.

— Turning refusals into acceptances —

This might seem odd but you can often adapt a refusal to become an acceptance, albeit of something new. For example, you might have to refuse to take your friend's children to school every day because it would make you late for work. But you could offer to look after them for one Saturday a month to give your friend the chance to do her shopping and go to her riding lesson. It will also help you by giving your own children some friends to play with while you do your painting. By doing so you are making a positive contribution to your friendship but are not compromising your own priorities.

This idea can also be used at work. For example, if you cannot do that overtime for Pete tonight but have time in a few days to do some research for his report to the chairman, then offer to do so. Pete will be grateful and you can use some of the research in your own project. You might even get a mention when Pete's report reaches the chairman.

— Ways to say 'no' without tears —

Now that you have geared yourself up to saying no with confidence, I'll leave you with ten ways of saying no without leaving the other person aggrieved. Remember, saying no saves time so don't be afraid to say so.

1 No, but next week we can ...
2 No, but why don't I ...
3 No, I won't be free until ...
4 No, I've already got to finish ...
5 No, I'm afraid that I have to ...
6 No, I'm sorry but I can't ...
7 No, unfortunately I ...
8 No, but could you ask me again in ...
9 No, but I could ...
10 No, it isn't possible now but ... .

If after all this you still find the word no hard to use, break yourself in gently. Here are some other ways to refuse politely but firmly:

1 I'm sorry, but ...
2 Unfortunately that won't be possible because ...
3 I'm afraid that ...
4 That's lovely, but ...
5 I'd have liked to but ...
6 I normally would do but ... (if it's true).

TOP TEN TIPS

1 Believe you have the right to say no.
2 Be firm but pleasant.
3 Practise saying no in front of a mirror.
4 Smile while you refuse.
5 Don't say yes to fill a silence.
6 Be honest.
7 Offer an alternative, if you can.
8 Say thank you when appropriate.
9 Ask for time to think – if you really need it.
10 Trust your instincts.

Summary

Learning to say no is one of the most important time management techniques. Only say yes to requests that fit in with your own priorities. Say no politely but firmly – look at some of the examples in this chapter. If the other person won't take no for an answer keep repeating your refusal in different ways until they get the message. Say what you mean and don't forget to say thank you when it is deserved. Agree a workload and timetable for extra jobs with your boss. Help out colleagues when you can but not to the detriment of your own work.

7

REDUCE PAPERWORK

Less paper means more useful time to spare. This chapter dispels the myth of the paperless office and explains how to reduce paper to the absolute minimum. It describes how to deal with incoming paper efficiently and effectively and how to reduce the amount that you yourself produce.

— The myth of the paperless office —

Like many people today I work with wonderful machines – a computer, photocopier, fax. They make my working life easier but the one thing they don't do is reduce the amount of paper I have to deal with.

But the myth of the paperless office still remains. The theory is that machines have made paper obsolete. We can communicate by phone, fax, e-mail, teleprinter – paper needn't exist. So why do we still find ourselves surrounded by pieces of paper?

The answer is that we have built paper into our way of working whether it is necessary or not. We word process our letters and other documents and then print out one or more copies for reference or posting. We talk on the phone and then send written confirmation. When salespeople call we get rid of them by asking for details to be sent by post instead. We send letters by e-mail and then make printed copies of the replies. We photocopy all kinds of documents because it is easy to do so. We send copies of documents and letters to other people 'for your files' or 'for your information'. We receive similar amounts in return. And where do we put it? In files, on the floor, on shelves, in cupboards – anywhere there is space. There is always too much.

—— What paper do you need? ——

You might be one of those exceptionally tidy people without a piece of paper in sight. But even you, I suspect, do not actually need all the paper you have neatly filed away.

Before you do anything else you need to decide what exactly you need to keep paper for. You might be keeping it for any or all of the following reasons:

- reference
- interest
- as vital to your work
- no particular reason – you can't think what else to do with it
- the papers from that source have always been kept
- the company demands three copies of everything
- it might come in handy
- to read when you have time
- to pass on to colleagues.

Actually, most paper you keep is unnecessary. With some thought you can eliminate or reduce the paperwork in your life.

TIME MANAGEMENT TIP

Not sure whether a document should be kept for reference? Put it in a box for three months. If nobody has asked to see it, throw it away.

The paper you must keep

Some paper is too important to throw away. You must keep legal documents, for example. You must also keep financial records for seven years. Some personnel and company documents need to be kept for reference. If you are not sure which documents come in this category in your company, ask your line manager for clarification. These documents can usually be stored safely in a central archive. But don't take everything at face value. If you can't see the value of keeping certain documents and your company can't give you a good reason for keeping them, suggest that they are unnecessary. You will save yourself and the company a lot of storage space!

A tidy workplace is an efficient workplace

The more paper you deal with each day and the more paper you keep, the more difficult it is to work efficiently. Time gets wasted not just dealing with the paper but looking for the bits that you do need. You know you have the contract somewhere, but where? Instead of dealing with it immediately you have to spend time looking for it. On average office workers spend three-quarters of an hour or more a day looking for papers. That's before they deal with it.

So, the prime requirements are less paper, a tidy workplace and dealing with paper efficiently and effectively. By knowing what to do with paper when it arrives in your hands, where to put it if you do keep it and how to deal with it effectively you can save time and improve your work patterns.

Clearance action plan

The best way to make a start on your paper problems is to start immediately. Choose a time when you can spend at least half an hour on the project. Aim to complete it over several days. Don't try to do it all in one long go. You will just get tired and frustrated.

First, assemble your paper clearance tools:

- one or more large wastepaper bins
- four large cardboard boxes
- labels
- files and folders
- marker pens.

Before you start, label your boxes 'no idea', 'pass on', 'action' and 'filing'. The box labelled 'no idea' will be filled with all those papers that you don't know what to do with, or even what they are for. Eventually you will be able to find a place for all of them, but at the moment put them in this box.

The 'pass on' box is not for corpses but for those papers that should or could be dealt with by other people. And the 'action' box is for paper that you must deal with – in fact your work. The 'filing' box is going to contain all papers that absolutely must be kept. Naturally, all rubbish goes in your wastepaper bin.

The trick about clearing paper is to deal with it one piece at a time. Some books tell you to strip your desk of everything and then deal with the paper. It is much better to work through methodically, otherwise you are just moving the problem from the desk to the floor.

Pick up the first piece of paper on your desk that your hand lands on. Look at it carefully. You can do several things with it – deal with it, pass it on, file it or throw it away. Put it in the relevant box or the wastepaper bin. It should be obvious what each piece of paper is for. If you really cannot decide, put it in the 'no idea' box. Later you will empty this one too.

Keep working around your desk until all the paper on it has been dealt with. Include anything else that is made of paper – magazines, reports, stationery, books, etc. Put them in the relevant place, for example, on a bookshelf. If you are keeping magazines, tear out only the articles you need and throw the rest away. Put stationery in a desk drawer. Continue until the desk is clear of paper.

— What do you need on your desk? —

You will probably find that your desk still has things on it that are not made of paper. You might have any or all of the following:

- computer
- fax
- scanner
- pens/pencils
- photos
- telephone

- answering machine
- coffee/tea mug
- food
- plastic paper trays
- clock
- executive toy
- paper-clips/rubber bands/drawing pins, etc.
- paperweight
- diary
- electronic organiser.

If possible, move any electronic equipment off your desk. Your computer must stay, so must your phone. But a computer tower could go on the floor, the printer, scanner and fax could go on another desk and your electronic organiser should be locked away unless it is in use. If possible, ask your company technical team to network your computer to the company system so that you can use a common printer. Get them to fix an internal fax card to your computer. Flatbed scanners can safely go on the floor.

If your desk does not contain enough drawers or cupboards or is not suitable for your needs, see if you can get it changed. If you cannot do so because of company policy (e.g. only the director gets a useful-sized desk with the necessary extras) then improvise. Put a small filing cabinet under one side of your desk to take stationery and other bits and pieces. If you have your own office and there is enough room, why not buy yourself a dedicated computer desk? These can now be bought very cheaply from office stores and will take care of all your computer storage problems and clear your main desk for other work.

Pens, pencils, paper-clips can go in a plastic holder, while everything else – stapler, notebooks, ruler, etc – goes in your desk drawer.

When you put the essential equipment on your desk, remove anything else. That executive toy might be cute, but it's not businesslike. Take it home to amuse the family. Coffee cups, food, and non-essentials should be banished to where they belong. Be ruthless about returning them each time you have finished with them. And should you be eating at your desk anyway?

You might regularly be given commemorative paperweights or other advertising curios. Use the most recent paperweight and give the rest to your staff. Take advertising gimmicks home or throw them away.

By the time you have finished reading this chapter you won't have much paper left to need weighing down!

It would be cruel to forbid you to personalise your desk in some way. We all like to feel that our desk is ours. But limit yourself to one family photo. Flowers can go on a windowsill or shelf.

TIME MANAGEMENT TIP

If you or your staff regularly receive gifts of pens and/or paper, collect them in a centrally placed box and consider donating them to a local school.

What papers on your desk?

Now you have disposed of all the paper on your desk and left just the most important pieces of equipment, what paper should be on your desk? You should only have the paper you are immediately working on. Everything else should be filed away. Books should be on a shelf. Your diary can either be on your desk or in your desk drawer. And that's it. That's all you need on your desk.

Close to your desk or in a desk filing drawer you will need your daily, weekly and monthly files (as discussed later in this chapter). You will only need to take out the relevant files when you are working on them or referring to them at the beginning of the day/week/month.

Where to put the rest?

Now look into your four boxes. Go through your 'pass on' box, marking the name of the person it has to go to on the top. Your secretary can pass these on to the relevant people immediately. The 'filing' box is obvious – file each piece of paper in its relevant file. The 'action' box contains papers that you should deal with as soon as possible. Sort them in order of priority, put them in a folder, put the folder on your desk and deal with it as soon as you have finished clearing up. Finally, the 'no idea' box. If you really have no idea what to do with it, then it probably isn't worth keeping. If you can't bring yourself to throw any of it away, ask your secretary or a colleague to go through it and decide for you. Sometimes it pays to let someone else do the dirty work.

Any articles torn from a magazine to read later can be put in a separate folder. Put this in your briefcase and read them when you have some transition time – waiting for an appointment, travelling on a train, etc. When you have read an article, throw it away. Do not keep it unless you are sure you will need to refer to it again. Remember, articles are quickly out of date so there is rarely a need to keep them for long.

Books should go on a bookshelf. If there are many large volumes that you only use occasionally, which the office could share, put them in a communal place.

Incoming paper

You've now sorted out the paper you already have but what happens to the paper that comes each day, whether by post or other means? You must use the same system to deal with it as you did with existing paper.

Look at each piece in turn. There are four things you can do with them. Throw it away, file it, pass it on or do something with it. Do you really need to keep it or can you pass it on? Throw it away? Does it need to be filed – if so, do you need to keep it or can it go in the general office filing system? If it needs to be acted on must it be dealt with now or later? If so, mark its priority on top and put it on your desk. Deal with it and your other papers in the priority order marked.

Sometimes when dealing with post you don't need to look at it at all. If it is obviously junk mail, throw it straight into the bin. Just be careful that it is junk mail and not that cheque you've been waiting for.

The wastepaper bin secret

A good tip for dealing with junk paper of any kind when it arrives is to have a wastepaper bin in every room, whether at your office or at home. That way you have no excuse for not throwing rubbish away as soon as it reaches you. It will also stop paper stacking up on any available surface. I work from home so every room in my house contains a large red office wastepaper bin. Unnecessary paper can be junked wherever I find it.

Have wastepaper bins in every place that you might look at paper. By your desk and those of your secretary and staff, by the photocopier, by the filing cabinet, beside the armchair you sit in to read your papers. By the front door at home. If you do not have immediate means of getting rid of paper, it tends to get left on surfaces until it forms piles. If a wastepaper bin is always to hand then you have no excuse for not junking unwanted paper immediately.

If you want to make your recycling credentials clear, have two bins at each point – a large wastepaper basket for recycling paper that can be collected and put in the recycling area later and a small bin for other rubbish.

Why not suggest that your company invests in large green wastepaper bins marked with the recycling logo and the company logo. If these are placed where I suggest, the amount of unwanted paper should be reduced immediately and the recycling programme will benefit.

Recycling

The ideal place for any unwanted paper nowadays is the recycling bin. If your company already has an arrangement with a paper recycling firm to collect waste paper regularly, all you need do is ensure that your unwanted paper is put in the right container at the right time. Otherwise see what can be recycled. Keep a recycling box or bin where it is easy to dump unwanted paper. Contact a paper recycling firm to see if they can make a regular collection from your company's premises. If not, perhaps you could take a sack a week to the nearest recycle centre on your way home.

TIME MANAGEMENT TIP

If your company produces a lot of cardboard and paper, consider investing in a baling machine to make storage of the bales easier.

Only touch it once

Time management books that tell you not to handle a piece of paper more than once are being unrealistic. That is an ideal situation. In practice you might need to handle it twice or even three times to complete a piece of work. But if you find that you are constantly picking up and putting down the same piece of paper or document, take time to deal with it in depth. Give yourself a time limit for dealing with it and then dispose of it.

TIME MANAGEMENT TIP

Put a red dot on a piece of paper every time you pick it up. Three dots – deal with it now!

— Stop paper before it gets to you —

One way to reduce your paper load and save time is to stop unnecessary papers ever reaching you in the first place. Think of simple ways to achieve this.

First, get your name taken off junk mail lists. Write to the Mail Preference Service (see Useful Addresses). It takes a few months for this to be effective but eventually your junk mail intake should reduce.

Next, take your name off any internal mail lists that are not absolutely vital. You might enjoy receiving several magazines and all the internal memos but if you don't need to see them, take your name off. Lydia found that she was on so many internal lists that the amount of paperwork she had to read at the end of each day was more than she could get through in a week. She took her name off all lists except those directly concerned with her work. The paper load reduced dramatically and she did not miss any of the papers she no longer received.

Don't ask people to send you faxes or write you letters 'just for confirmation' unless they are vital. Incidentally, the same applies to e-mail and computer faxes. Just because they are on a computer doesn't mean they are not junk mail. Responding to e-mail can take a disproportionate amount of time out of your day if you don't take steps to limit it.

Probably the biggest producer of paper is the photocopier. It is all too easy to run off lots of copies of practically anything made of paper on the grounds of 'we might as well send so-and-so a copy just to be on the safe side' or 'just to keep them informed' or 'we'd better keep a copy of that, in case anyone wants to see it'. Don't do it. You only need to photocopy something if the original is vital and you need to replace it or you are producing several copies for a specific reason. If at all possible do not photocopy anything. You rarely need several copies of letters. The original usually suffices, as long as it is stored centrally. You can now get computer filing programs that can store and file scanned documents on your computer. Why not invest in one of those and eliminate paper letter files altogether?

Any letters or documents that must be kept for legal reasons or for future reference should be moved to a central archive. The date when they can be destroyed should be prominently marked on each folder or box. Once every three months send a member of staff to check these dates and destroy any of those on which the date has passed.

Filing for fun

Part of the way you control paper is to ensure that it is put where you can find it and that the papers you need are to hand. Now you have eliminated as much existing and incoming paper as possible, turn your hand to reorganising your filing system.

First of all label your files according to the broadest category that is useful, such as accounts, newsletters, suppliers, personnel, health, training, sales, etc. Put groupings within these alphabetically, using nouns or names as the labels, for example use company and individual names (by surname) or the main noun of any phrase. Always put the most recent documents in front.

Alphabetise

You have already put your files in alphabetical order. Now alphabetise everything else that you can – books, articles torn from magazines and filed, folders, labelled boxes. In fact, put into alphabetical order anything that lends itself to this method. This might seem a very basic system but it is simple, effective and easily remembered.

TIME MANAGEMENT TIP

Show your secretary how your filing system works. If possible, introduce it to your staff so that everyone can quickly find documents from any system if someone is away.

—— 'Bring forward' systems ——

You need a system for reminding yourself of future actions and for keeping papers you need to deal with at a future date accessible.

You will write future appointments in your diary but you can also use it for recording when action has to be taken and when deadlines have to be met. It can also be used for recording the stages of a project or work in progress. In your diary put:

- renewal dates
- repetitive tasks
- project starting dates
- lists of materials for meetings.

TIME MANAGEMENT TIP

A 12-month diary or planner might not be adequate for recording all forward dates and renewals. Use an 18-month diary or have next year's diary to hand.

You need to co-ordinate this with the paperwork that goes with each of these. The simplest 'bring forward' method of all is to use your diary and one folder. For any future action or appointment, note the date in your diary and list the papers you will need. Put the papers in one folder. Papers for other dates can be added to the folder in date order. When the day arrives, remove the relevant papers.

To remind yourself of action to be taken, put a reminder into your diary a few days or a week before the relevant date.

This system is adequate for a simple work style, but many people need something that will cope with much more paperwork. In that case, you need a comprehensive but simple 'bring forward' system of filing so that related paperwork is kept safe and accessible.

For this you need 12 folders labelled with the months of the year and 31 folders labelled with the day's dates of 1 to 31.

When you receive a piece of paper or document that needs to be dealt with at a future date, put it in the relevant month. At the end of the current month sort the next month's folder contents into the relevant numbered folder. Deal with each day's work as appropriate.

If you need prior warning of something that needs to be done, put a note in an earlier day or month folder allowing enough time for preparation. Or open a 'next week' folder.

This 'bring forward' system should be quite adequate for keeping most papers under control. If you need a more sophisticated system, include weekly folders.

Your diary or management planner will contain details of important dates that you can synchronise with your folders.

Other folders and files that you might need are personnel files. These might be for staff or clients. Put information and action memos in these files. Then you will have all the information to hand when dealing with a particular person.

Your monthly, weekly and daily folders should all be in your desk filing drawer so that you can reach them easily and quickly.

— Reduce your own paper output —

You should encourage other people not to use and store so much paper too. Look at what you send out to people and think of ways of cutting down. Try these:

- write a reply on the bottom of memos/letters and return it
- keep anything you write brief and readable
- phone a reply
- e-mail
- keep letters/proposals to one side of paper
- send copies to fewer people

- reduce forms
- reduce instruction manuals.

Letter writing made easy

The advice is to keep letters short and easy to read but many people find writing letters difficult. They waste a lot of time agonising over how to express themselves on paper.

You don't want to spend too much time on writing letters, although it is a large part of many people's jobs. If you have letters to write, do the following:

- file letters you have to reply to in two folders – high and low priority
- answer high-priority letters first; save low-priority letters for spare moments
- gather any information you need beforehand
- when replying to a letter, deal with the points in the order they were made
- keep to one point in each paragraph, even if the paragraph is only one sentence long
- if composing a letter, list the points you want to make
- keep language simple and sentences short
- if it is too late to write, phone.

TIME MANAGEMENT TIP

Keep a pile of stamped postcards in your drawer or briefcase. Use them instead of letters when only a brief personal reply is required.

Forms

Collect all the forms that you and your staff have to fill in or send out during a month. Look at them and ask yourself 'what would happen if this form didn't exist?' Often the answer would be 'not very much'. Try eliminating one or two forms and seeing what the consequence is. If life goes on much as before, do not reintroduce them.

For forms that do prove vital look at how they are set out and the language they use. Can the form be rewritten and restyled to be made simpler, clearer, shorter? If so, redesign it.

Far too much time is wasted in many workplaces completing forms that have no value or no real purpose. Most people do not need the constant check of form filling to ensure that they do their job well or that basic procedures are being adhered to. If they do, their line manager or supervisor is usually adequate check. Eliminate as many forms as you can. Most people can be trusted to follow general guidelines. In many cases sensible approximation is required rather than exactitude. Follow the well-known Marks and Spencer doctrine 'When in doubt, throw it out'.

Company instruction manuals

How often have you or your staff had to wade through thick instruction manuals? Company instruction manuals should be as short and to the point as possible. Staff are more likely to read and remember a short clear booklet than an inch-thick tome. If your company is very large, provide one slim booklet for each section.

Using machines

It is possible to eliminate much of the paper we produce by using computers but few people seem willing to do this. Pieces of paper seem secure and the computer might crash, wiping out anything saved on it. The answer to the latter fear is, of course, to do what all computer manuals and experts advise and few people actually do. Regularly back up your work onto disk. This is a familiar procedure and if you follow it there is no reason why most of your 'paperwork' shouldn't be created and kept on your computer. You can use e-mail to communicate in place of letters or faxes straight onto a computer screen.

TIME MANAGEMENT TIP

When replying to e-mail, put any action into the subject line, for example, 'need reply by Thursday a.m.'

Whole documents can be sent by attaching them electronically to either of these methods. Documents can be scanned into your computer and arranged into files and folders as if they were on paper and just as easily retrieved. Your work can be created and stored on any computer and sent to anyone with a compatible system of communication. So why use paper at all?

Other paper-based products now appear as standard in computer software programs – organisers, diaries, calendars, account sheets, database listings, etc. If you really want to eliminate paper from your world then spend time studying your computer's manuals to find out what it is capable of. Ask your company's computer technician to advise you and show you how to use it to the best advantage. Invest in new software or computer upgrades if this will enable you to take advantage of the more advanced programs.

Incidentally, do not be put off by technical jargon. Ask someone to explain it to you in plain language and give a demonstration. Or sign up for an evening class in computer use. Using computers is straightforward once you understand the basics. If I can do it, you can!

TIME MANAGEMENT TIP

Choose software with on-screen demonstrations – it is easier to understand a demonstration.

Use the phone

Before you create paper for other people to deal with, think. You want to communicate in the quickest and most time-saving way possible that is suitable for the nature of the transaction. Can you phone instead of writing a letter? If you keep to the point (see Chapter 8) a phone call can be quicker and more productive. Can you use a tape recorder to dictate letters, record memos and note ideas? These can then be typed up in one session by your secretary. Can you visit the person you need to communicate with? Think of ways to get the message across without using paper at all.

Of course some things, such as contracts, must be printed out and kept. But you will be surprised at how much other paperwork can be eliminated entirely. And the less paper in your office or home, the more time you will save by not having to deal with it.

TOP TEN TIPS

1 Accept that no office is going to be paperless.
2 Keep legal and financial documents safely.
3 File it, pass it on, act on it or throw it away.
4 Clear your desk.
5 Keep only necessary papers to hand.
6 Touch each piece of paper once or twice only.
7 Reduce the amount of paper reaching you.
8 Have a simple filing system and use it.
9 Use as few pieces of paper as possible.
10 Use machines to eliminate paper.

Summary

Clear your desk of all paper one piece at a time. Either file it, pass it on, throw it away or act on it. Eliminate as much incoming paper as possible. Reduce your own output. Use a broad simple filing system and encourage everyone in the office to use the same system. Use monthly and daily files to keep track of future projects. Wherever possible use your computer to eliminate paperwork.

8

SUBDUE YOUR PHONE

This chapter explains why making and receiving phone calls is so time consuming. It shows that using the phone a lot is not a guarantee of more efficiency and gives you techniques for reducing your phone calls.

Phones waste time

If you think that the more phone calls you make and receive the more effective you are being, think again. Using the phone can be a very time-wasting occupation. All the while you are using the phone you are not getting on with other work. Often the temptation to indulge in a little social gossip while on the phone is too strong to resist. Many phone calls are unnecessary or stray from the point. And while you are on the phone your staff can't consult you, your colleagues can't liaise with you and other more important contacts cannot reach you.

The phone is a necessary tool for any workplace in this modern age – that is undeniable. When something needs to be decided quickly or a point needs to be clarified then a phone call can sort that out quickly. But for the rest of the time phone calls are largely superfluous.

Both incoming and outgoing calls can be time wasting. People phone you for a chat when you have urgent work on hand, or don't get to the point quickly. Think about the calls you make that are unnecessary or the times you try again and again to get through but cannot. All types of phone calls should be judged by how effectively they contribute to the work you have to do. If they don't, they need to be eliminated or reduced.

So, what can you do to make your use of the phone more effective?

—————— Keep a phone log ——————

You need to know exactly what kind of calls you are making and receiving and at what times of day they usually take place. Once you have this information you can streamline your calls so that you not only save time but use the time on the phone more effectively. To do this you need to keep a phone log.

A phone log is simply a piece of paper on which you record the time any phone call starts and finishes, who is making the call and why. You can add comments too. You can keep separate logs for incoming and outgoing calls and add comments if you wish. Start now and keep a log for at least a week, two or more weeks if possible. Try to choose a typical week. That will give you a clear idea of how much time you are spending on the phone and whether the calls were necessary. (See Figure 8.)

By looking at the telephone log for incoming calls you can see who phones you and how often. You will frequently find that the same person tends to phone you at similar times. You can also see whose calls are most irritating and time wasting.

But that is only part of the story. You should also keep a telephone log of all your outgoing calls. The results will probably surprise you. I expect you think that you are efficient about using the phone and that your calls are short. But what about that call to Barry when you followed up a brief discussion about some work with a longer chat about last week's football match? Or the pleasant but unnecessary call to your partner? Keeping a log of your own calls will produce some surprises and show you where you can reduce calls.

Figure 9 shows you how easy it is to waste time when making your own calls, however efficient you think you normally are. Keeping a log of your outgoing calls can be a revelation.

Analyse your calls

Once you have spent at least a week noting your calls, take a look at your phone logs. You should immediately be able to see who is making

Date and time	Caller	Organisation	Reason for call	Length of call (mins)	How often calls made	Comments
2nd May 9.30 a.m.	Sally Clarke PA to RT	XYZ Motors	To check on delivery for Friday	5 mins	Twice a month	Pleasant person who keeps to the point and only phones when necessary.
9.42 a.m.	John Truman Salesman	Walter & Co	To ask for meeting to show new product	10 mins	First phone call from this man	Irritating person who tried to give me a sales pitch over the phone – arranged a meeting but then had to cut him off
10.03 a.m.	Mrs Smith Charles's PA	Egbert Manufacturing	Asked me to send Charles a copy of the tender	2 mins	Two or three times a month	Brisk and cheerful – never wastes a call.
10.17 a.m.	Ms R Brown PR	Fulsome Enterprises	Read out press release for my approval	12 mins	About once every two or three weeks	Frequency of calls depends on what is newsworthy – very nice but tends to want to chat.
10.48 a.m.	Tony (my husband)		Reminded me to collect theatre tickets	3 mins	About once a week, but often not for a month	I've told him only to phone in emergencies but he likes to phone if he thinks I'll forget something.

Figure 8 Telephone log for incoming calls

the most time-wasting calls to you and also those people you make calls to that are unnecessary or overlong. Your comments will show you whether the time wasting is your fault or theirs – and we all waste time on phones occasionally. Now that you have the information it is time to work out how to organise your calls so that you waste the least possible time and yet still remain effective.

Date and time	Who call was to	Reason for call	Length of call (mins)	How often calls made	Comments
4th May 8.45	Secretary	To ask her to find conference papers for my arrival	2 mins	Frequently	Usually calls are brief and to the point.
9.10	Derek, accounts	Checking my last salary statement	8 mins	Rarely	I suppose I could have left a message.
9.24	Alan, boss	Confirming change of meeting	10 mins	At least once a day	I often have several things to say - I should deal with them all at once.
10.47	Secretary	Asking her to send copy of new agenda to Alan	1 min	Frequently	To the point.
11.17	Mr Jaques	About Euro grant	25 mins	Only second call to Mr Jaques but expect to speak to him more frequently	We had a lot to discuss but kept to the issues - Mr J very businesslike.

Figure 9   Telephone log for outgoing calls

Dealing with incoming calls

Now that you know who wastes your time when they phone you, who is unpleasant and who you really need to talk to you can start to control your incoming calls.

Take calls at specified times

You do not want incoming calls at all hours of the day otherwise your work will be constantly interrupted. So the first time-saving rule is to ask callers to phone during certain times. This eliminates the constant interruptions that plague your day. You will see from your logs that some people tend to phone you at certain times so you can allow for this in your work schedule.

So, for example, you might decide to receive calls between 10 a.m. and 11 a.m. and 3 p.m. and 4 p.m. daily. Or you might ask people to phone you on certain days, for example, Monday or Wednesday afternoons or Friday morning. The rest of the time your answer machine will be on or your secretary or a member of staff will take messages for you to respond to later.

Have information ready

Next, when you know someone will be calling you about a particular subject, have all the information to hand so that when they do make contact you can answer them straight away. The information might be on paper or oral reports from other people. They might be anywhere in the company. Gather the information in good time so that when you get the call you don't have to waste time searching for answers.

Limit the time

Make it clear to all callers that you have limited time. State at the start of the call 'I can give you five minutes' and then finish the call after that time.

Let your secretary deal with calls

Give your secretary permission to deal with most incoming calls. Decide who you must speak to – your boss, your partner, Derek from XYX Co and ask your secretary to deal with everything else. They can deal with straightforward problems and take messages that you can deal with in one time block later.

Don't take transferred calls

Discourage colleagues from transferring calls to you. Make it clear that you will only take transferred calls from certain people and that everyone else must deal with their own calls. On the other hand, if you think that a colleague rather than yourself has the relevant expertise the caller needs, transfer the call to your colleague. Tell your secretary what types of calls to transfer and to whom they should be transferred.

Check that your company switchboard knows which calls should be transferred where and that unsuitable calls are not directed to you out of habit.

Don't answer the phone

A little-used method of cutting down on incoming calls is to leave the phone to ring. This takes practise because people instinctively want to answer phones immediately. Obviously, if your company has issued instructions that all calls are to be answered within so many rings, then you must abide by that. Your secretary should field most unnecessary calls in any case and that rule will mostly apply to her.

If you have leeway about answering calls, do not pick up the phone immediately. Finish the work and then answer. Or leave your answer machine on loud enough to hear the caller's message so you can decide whether to answer now or ring back later. Phones that display the caller's phone number are useful because it gives you an indication of who is calling.

TIME MANAGEMENT TIP

Remember that all phone calls must be answered – but not necessarily by you.

─────────────── **Taking notes** ───────────────

Make sure that you, your secretary and your staff know how to take good messages from phone calls. Use a specially designed phone message sheet to ensure that no vital information is lost. Listen carefully to the caller and find out what they really want before trying to answer them. Take full notes so that you can refer back to them and can initiate action from them. If you want your secretary to deal with calls for you, make sure that their note-taking skills have been learnt well.

```
┌─────────────────────────────────────────────────────────────────┐
│  ┌──┐   TELEPHONE MESSAGE FOR _____   │
│  │▓▓│                                                            │
│  └──┘   OF (DEPT/SECTION) _____ │
│                                                                   │
│         DATE   _____  TIME _____   │
│                                                                   │
│  MESSAGE TAKEN BY _____  │
│                                                                   │
│  CALLER'S NAME _____  │
│                                                                   │
│  OF _____   │
│                                                                   │
│  TELEPHONE NUMBER _____  │
│                                                                   │
│  MESSAGE _____   │
│  _____  │
│  _____  │
│  ACTION _____   │
│  _____  │
│    ☐              ☐                  ☐                            │
│  URGENT        WILL CALL LATER      PLEASE CALL BACK              │
└─────────────────────────────────────────────────────────────────┘
```

Figure 10 Telephone message pad

Any action to be taken should be noted on the message sheet. If the person who has taken the message can deal with it (your secretary, a colleague, a member of your staff) they should be empowered to do so. You should only be given the sheet when action needs to be taken by you. Your secretary, of course, should list the messages daily and note any action that was taken and by whom, for your information.

Make sure that any message sheet you design or that your company provides is large enough to take all the information and contains enough room for the message and action information. You will not save time if you have to search for another piece of paper because the sheet is too small.

Put copies of the phone message pad where everyone can see them and will use them, for example next to every phone, including your own. Instruct everyone to use them.

If you want to be sure that messages are not mislaid, the telephone message sheet could be printed in a carbon block so that there is always a second copy. Once action has been taken both copies can be destroyed.

TIME MANAGEMENT TIP

If your telephone messages keep getting lost use a carbon-copy pad. Throw the spare copies away once the pad has been used.

Unwanted calls

Some of your calls will be from people you don't want to speak to. These might include someone who has dialled a wrong number to a telephone salesperson who won't take no for an answer; from someone phoning just for a chat to an aggressive caller demanding you solve a problem. Whatever the reason you don't want their calls, you need to keep calm and be polite, however irritating or rude they are. At the same time you want to discourage their calls and get them off the line as quickly as possible. Unwanted calls are great time wasters unless you know how to deal with them effectively.

Getting rid of chatty callers

Other people don't seem to care that your time is valuable. If they have a problem and want to talk about it at length or just phone for a chat, they can waste a lot of your time unless you are firm with them. But at the same time you have to be polite.

If it is someone you know well you can simply say 'I can't talk now, Sally, can you call me back in a couple of hours' (or whenever is convenient). However, this will not work with someone who will not take no for an answer. Rob, a health council worker, has a good technique for dealing with these types of caller. 'Don't say anything positive, not even "er" or "but". That just encourages them. Don't respond. Wait until they have said everything they want to and come to a stop. Don't say anything for three or four seconds after that. They'll get nervous and start speaking again. But if you repeat the trick several times they will eventually give up.'

Malicious calls

You might be unlucky enough to be on the receiving end of malicious or abusive calls if the callers have got past your secretary. If so, put the phone down immediately and inform your line manager and also the telephone company which will have a system for dealing with this type of call. If the caller sounds threatening or dangerous, call the police too.

Help lines

If you are constantly having to deal with calls relating to problems that could be dealt with elsewhere, consider asking whether your company could introduce one or more dedicated phone lines where the calls are dealt with by specially trained staff. These staff can deal with most of the calls and pass on difficult calls immediately to the person most suited to deal with them.

Getting rid of callers politely

For the general run of calls that are inconvenient and potentially time wasting, here are some tricks that will help you get rid of them without being rude. But remember that you are supposed to present a helpful and efficient image of yourself and your company, so be careful not to use these inappropriately.

Don't ask the caller to:

- send a letter or fax, or
- send more information (or you will increase your incoming paper).

Instead, ask the caller to:

- try again later (and then be unavailable the rest of the day)
- try someone else in the organisation (get the caller transferred to someone who can help).

You can also tell the caller that:

- you are not interested (for persistent salesmen and other thick-skinned callers)
- you have only 30 seconds left (for callers with whom you are losing patience. After 30 seconds say 'I'm going to put the phone down now' – and do so)
- you can't make a decision now. Don't be rushed into making a decision over the phone without consideration
- you'll call back later – but only if you mean it.

A final, effective way of ending an unwanted phone call is simply to say 'goodbye' in the middle of the conversation. This confuses the caller who won't know whether they said anything that implied the conversation was ending. They might be puzzled or hurt but are unlikely to remain cross because they won't be sure it wasn't their fault.

—— Dealing with outgoing calls ——

As you control your outgoing calls you have a lot of scope for doing so in the most time-efficient manner, and also for improving their effectiveness.

First of all, decide whether you really need to make the call. Can you visit the person, send a fax or e-mail, get someone else to deal with it? In fact, in many cases a call is unnecessary and it would be better to do nothing at all.

Planning your calls

If you have decided that you must make calls there are many ways to ensure that you can save time and make the calls efficiently. Whenever you think a call is necessary, take a little time to plan before you reach for the phone.

The most time-efficient way of dealing with outgoing phone calls is to make them all (or at least most of them) during one or two specific times of the day. You can then deal with them in one go, then get on with other things. Choose times when you are most likely to find people in and when you have enough free time to deal with all the calls together.

Before you make any call decide what you are going to say and how you are going to say it. These points will help you:

- know exactly to whom you want to speak
- know what you want to say
- prepare a message in case the person you want is out
- have the relevant paperwork at hand
- have paper and pen ready
- have important facts and dates written down
- relax by breathing deeply
- visualise the person to whom you will be speaking
- picture a calming situation
- choose an appropriate time to call.

If you have to make a difficult call, don't put it off. Prepare yourself as above and then make the call as soon as you can. Get to the point quickly – neither of you will be helped if you dither.

Notes beforehand

Nothing wastes more time when you are making a call than having to search for information while you are on the phone.

Before you make any call, gather all the information you need. Do you need statistics, names and addresses, the last letter you received from the caller? Make sure that everything is by the phone when you make the call. That way you can answer queries on the spot.

Making notes

Make notes to yourself before you phone. List all the points that you want to make and answers to possible queries. Put them in order of priority so that the important points are made straight away. Keep a pen with you to make notes during the call.

Keep your calls short

To keep your own calls short, try these tips:

- keep a kitchen timer or clock by your phone, set it for five minutes and end the call when it rings

- don't say 'how are you?' and encourage chat
- give notice that you are ending the call by saying 'one last point ...'
- say you'll get back – and then keep the call short and to the point
- if all else fails, be rude (emergency use only!).

Organised calls – another example

Watch how other people organise their calls. Why not try Alice's method? Alice is a retail manager who has to deal with a great many phone calls every day. She has her own call-back action plan. She gives each call she receives a number and makes a note of the problem raised. At the end of the day she makes a numbered list of calls that either she or her secretary have to make and records details of the replies to be made. Each call is allocated a call sheet so that when the call is made a separate note of the reply or action to be taken is made for the files.

Phone workstation

It is a good idea to create your own phone workstation so that you do not have to search around for anything when either making or receiving calls. Make sure that your furniture is at the right height. This applies to whatever work you are doing, so simply altering the height of your chair or desk should increase your all-round comfort and efficiency.

Make sure that you have space on your desk for telephone call pads and note pads – you should have plenty of space if you tidied your desk as I suggested in Chapter 7. The pads should be permanently by your phone.

Many people put their phone down on their desk without thinking about whether it is in a sensible position. Which ear do you use for listening? Which hand do you pick the phone up with? When you pick up the phone do you:

- have to twist in your chair?
- find the cord gets tangled?
- have to reach over someone else to answer it?
- have to change it to the other hand?
- have to get up from your desk to answer it?

If you have any of these problems, your phone is in the wrong place. Move it to the side that is most convenient and involves you in the least movement but still allows you to take notes. You might want to put the phone in the middle of the back of your desk so that you can pick it up quickly with either hand.

A pin board above your desk is an effective way of keeping messages in view until dealt with but don't use it as another filing system just to get rid of paper.

Your secretary and staff should also rearrange their desks so that their phoning is made easier. It's no good you minimising your time on the phone if your staff aren't doing the same.

——— Phone call technology ———

Save time by making the most of the technology now available for dealing with calls.

Answer machine

This is the basic necessity. It can store phone messages until you want to deal with them. By turning the sound up you can hear the caller's message and decide whether it is urgent enough to pick up the phone and talk to them immediately.

There are additional useful phone services that can help you control your calls.

Call waiting

If someone phones you while you are already on the phone they hear a message asking them to hold, while you hear a bleep. You can put your original caller on hold to talk to the second caller or switch between the two.

Call diversion

Calls can be diverted to another extension, for example your secretary or another member of staff if you are working away from the office. This is a good way of ensuring uninterrupted time.

Call forwarding

This enables calls to reach you when you are working somewhere else, or if you can only use your mobile phone.

Call sequencing

This keeps callers in a queue until they can be dealt with.

Mobile and portable phones and pagers

Mobile phones and portable phones can be used wherever you are (mobile phones can be used in cars). Although convenient, you should not use them where they disturb others. Never use a mobile phone while driving; it is extremely dangerous.

You can see that modern technology can make using the phone much easier, as well as allowing to control your calls.

Voice mail

If you have a computer system that uses voice mail you can use your computer to store incoming calls until you feel like answering them. Don't forget to answer voice mail – allow time each day for working through your voice mail list.

If dealing with your voice mail takes too much of your time, use these methods:

- increase the playback speed (if your computer has this feature)
- limit the length of time people can leave a message
- limit the number of messages your voice mail box can hold
- if the message isn't relevant to you, transfer it
- delete messages when you have finished with them.

Consider installing two phone lines. If you expect to send or receive frequent faxes you might want a separate line for your fax machine. Alternatively, if your fax is connected to your computer and/or you can receive phone calls via your computer, you might want another phone line for your computer as well as your ordinary phone.

If you can only have one phone line you can get switching mechanisms that will recognise whether an incoming call is a fax or voice message and switch automatically to the relevant machine.

TOP TEN TIPS

1 Work out who phones you, why and when.
2 Take calls at specified times.
3 Keep calls short and to the point.
4 Don't make unnecessary calls.
5 Take full and accurate notes of any calls.
6 Make your workspace telephone friendly.
7 Use technology to deal with phone calls.
8 Prepare for calls – have all the paperwork to hand.
9 Smile – you can 'see' it down a phone line.
10 Always be polite – it may be the caller's only contact with your company.

Summary

Keep a phone log of incoming and outgoing calls to find out how much time you waste and who wastes it. Reduce incoming calls by using your secretary, an answer machine and by receiving calls only at certain times. Reduce outgoing calls by batching them and keeping them short and to the point. Use whatever phone services you find useful to deal with your calls more effectively. Use your time on the phone productively by preparing beforehand, listening effectively and taking complete notes.

9
MASTER YOUR MEETINGS

Meetings can be great time wasters. This chapter tells you how to reduce the amount of time you spend at meetings and how to streamline those that you have to attend.

── Meetings – work or waste? ──

If you are a typical employee a lot of your time will be taken up by meetings. Long meetings, short meetings, breakfast meetings, lunch meetings – you could (and some do) spend all day at meetings.

But many meetings are a complete waste of time. They are often dealing with things that could have been dealt with by other means or in other places and in less time. Others can be shortened without being less effective. Meetings are in fact one of the greatest time-wasting parts of the working day.

Think about how much meetings cost in terms of salary. Ten people in a meeting for one hour uses up ten working hours and the sum of one hours worth of salary from each of ten employees. If the meeting is attended by high-level employees, the cost to a company for that one meeting could be considerable.

More than one chairperson has decided to shock participants by telling them how much a meeting costs a company. Wendy, chairing the monthly board meeting, which usually overran in spite of her efforts, decided to teach the participants a lesson. She wrote the combined cost of their hourly worth (without the £ sign) on a white board. For every

20 minutes that the meeting overran because the participants wasted time, she quietly added another figure (20 minutes worth of salaried time). Eventually, as the figure grew larger, one of the participants asked what it meant. On being told that it was what the meeting had cost the company so far, there was a deadly silence. The next meeting was over in an hour!

Meetings waste time because many are unnecessary, ill-planned and/or have unclear objectives. Some take place in the wrong environment so that participants feel restless and are unable to concentrate. Others might have the wrong people at them or the right people absent. Yet more meetings have inadequate chairpersons or time management problems. Meetings like this waste time in many ways.

You do not have to be intimidated by meetings. One of the best ways of freeing time and becoming more productive is to cut down on meetings that serve no purpose and to streamline those that you have to go to.

— Eliminate unnecessary meetings —

The first step in eliminating unnecessary meetings is to take out your diary and look at the meetings that you have to go to during the next month and those that you have been to during the past month. How many of those were or are really necessary? Be honest, how many meetings were for the following reasons:

- the meeting is always held once a week/month/year
- to discuss a previous meeting
- to get people together
- to provide information
- to tell people what to do
- as a power ploy
- as a preliminary meeting.

Let's take a look at some of these. A lot of meetings are held because they've always been held. If you've inherited any of these regular meetings you should decide whether you actually need to continue attending or running them. If they do nothing except generate paper or are simply a talking shop, consider whether you could use the time more productively. Before you commit yourself to any regular meeting, find out exactly what the purpose is. Only go if it will be useful for your work.

If attendance by someone from your office is required, consider sending a member of your staff. Alternatively, if reading the minutes can keep you abreast of current events, ask for them to be sent to you. There is no law that says just because meetings are there you have to go to them.

You might be the culprit by instituting meetings that others have to attend. Before you do so, ask yourself whether you can always spare the time to get to them; if not, why should other people? Can you deal with the subject any other way – if you can, do so, don't organise regular meetings.

If your boss considers your attendance at certain meetings vital, then go to those but eliminate as many of the others as you can. Talk to your boss about the role of the meeting and discuss whether you need to attend each time.

Some meetings are arranged just to discuss the previous meeting. You know the kind – 'we just need to finish off discussing this – we need another meeting'. Why do you need to finish talking about it? Probably because the meeting was not run well enough for the discussion to take place within the time allowed. In that case you do not need those kinds of meetings. You need to ensure that meetings are efficiently run (see 'Managing meetings' later in this chapter).

Many meetings seem to be organised just so that people get together and have a chance to socialise. If this seems to be the case, suggest other better ways of doing this – perhaps a dinner once a month.

TIME MANAGEMENT TIP

If the meeting is the *only* time that participants can get together informally, allow a 20-minute 'social' break. But put it into the agenda and call time on it promptly.

If meetings are called to provide information, they are often duplicating other ways of doing so. Perhaps sending people written information, a promotional video or giving them a call would be a better and more efficient use of the time.

Meetings also exist for telling people what to do. The boss wants to tell you what to do and wants everyone else to hear. It can have a useful effect of introducing peer pressure, but more often just wastes time.

Meetings are notorious for the power struggles that go on in them. Georgette may call a meeting simply to prove that she has the power to do so and to show off her new project proposal. If you are not into power games, admire her proposal in a ten-minute chat and leave the meeting to its own devices.

Preliminary meetings are the quintessential waste of time. Either the subject is important enough to discuss and deal with now, or it isn't. A meeting to prepare for a meeting is a waste of time.

Don't let these meetings eat into your day. If you can't eliminate them, at least get out of attending them.

Don't go to meetings

If you can't stop unnecessary meetings, then avoid them. Here are some useful ploys to get out of attending meetings:

- send a member of your staff
- ask for a copy of the minutes
- send written comments for distribution
- ask for the meeting's secretary to send you a one-paragraph summary of action points
- be committed elsewhere.

Another reason for not going to meetings is because you have nothing to contribute. Why sit through a meeting if you have nothing to say? If this is the case, reading the minutes afterwards might give you all the information that you need.

—— Meetings by other means ——

If a group discussion seems necessary, think of other ways of dealing with it. If the responsibility is yours you can use these ideas, otherwise suggest them to the relevant chairperson.

Modern technology means that it is possible to hold meetings without leaving the building. You could hold a discussion with all the participants by telephone (teleconferencing) which can be arranged by the phone company. This is not only useful in large companies where everyone's time is valuable but also when participants live in distant parts of the country or abroad.

Another option which saves travelling time for people who would otherwise have to travel long distances is video conferencing. In this case, you can actually see the person you are taking to. You might be able to arrange this to take place in your own company building; otherwise the phone company can arrange it at special local centres.

Computers, too, can be set up so that communication is possible across vast distances. With a modem, access to the Internet and the right kind of software, you can 'talk' to people anywhere in the world by typing words onto the computer screen and reading the immediate reply.

To save time and tempers at these kinds of conferences, make sure that you and other participants prepare beforehand as if you were all meeting in one room. The same care in reading documents beforehand and having the relevant material to hand is just as necessary. You must agree a chairperson and secretary. Take time differences into account when making arrangements and start the meeting on time. It is even more important that the meeting is kept to the point because of the cost of using these systems.

Delegate the delegate

Don't go to meetings if you can send someone else. A properly briefed and equipped member of your staff might be the best person to send. They can report back to you in your own time and you can make any decisions in peace.

You would be failing in your duty if you did not give members of your staff the opportunity to go to meetings. They need to extend their experience and skills and you need staff who can step in when the situation requires and handle all kinds of situations. The more you empower your staff, the better they become and the more productive you will all be (see Chapter 10).

Make use of your staff's talents. Frances noticed that her personal assistant in the employment agency, Annie, was good at communicating and taking detailed notes. She gave Annie some training and sent her to the next area managers' meeting. Annie coped so well that she now attends all but a few meetings on Frances's behalf. Frances can rely on Annie to put her views forward and report back accurately. Her time is freed and Annie is benefiting from extending her work experience and is destined for a junior manager's role.

Managing meetings

By improving the way meetings are run, you can cut down the length of time they take and be more productive in them. If you are not in charge of the meeting you can make suggestions for improvement. Your own meetings can be run your way – effectively – by taking on board some of the ideas in this chapter.

What is a meeting for?

No meeting can be run effectively unless everyone has a clear idea about its purpose. Before you chair any meeting, decide what you want to achieve at the end of it. Usually meetings should result in some course of action being suggested. If you have called the meeting, what are you going to ask people to do at the end of it? Are you going to ask them to do something in particular? To consider and report on suggestions made at the meeting? To write reports? To give a talk at the next meeting? If you are attending the meeting, ask for clarification of these points at the start. If the discussion strays, remind everyone what the meeting is supposed to achieve and guide the discussion back to the point.

Whatever the purpose of your meeting, you should be clear about what you hope to achieve. You should also make it clear to all the participants both beforehand and at the start of the meeting exactly what you expect to achieve by the end and what you expect of them. Nobody attending should have any excuse for being unaware of what the meeting is for.

TIME MANAGEMENT TIP

Aim to accomplish three things in any one meeting.

The agenda

An agenda keeps a meeting on track and minds focused. Resist the temptation to add anything else that just occurs to you. Try to keep the agenda as short as possible while making sure that everything relevant has been included. Leave out anything that can be dealt with elsewhere or by other means. For example, if members need to be informed about the contents of a document, distribute copies beforehand with instructions that they are to be read before the meeting. Some information documents can be sent to people, with a list of names, on the 'tick when read and pass it on' basis.

The agenda should be distributed well in advance of the meeting to give everyone time to note the date in their diary and to prepare for it. Everything on the agenda should contribute to achieving the purpose of the meeting. If other people want to add items, do not let them unless the items are relevant. If they are concerned that their opinions will not be taken into account, arrange to deal with them on another occasion, perhaps by personal interview.

A good agenda should:

- explain any formalities clearly (such as the order of speakers, time limits on discussions)
- state where the meeting is to be held, the time and date and names of people attending
- mention any relevant business from previous meetings
- specify the subjects under discussion and explain what the meeting should achieve
- specify who will be leading discussions or presenting items on the agenda
- list the items in order
- state a firm starting and finishing time.

Chairing a meeting

A good chairperson can make or break a meeting. If you are in the chair, try to be a firm and effective chairperson. If participating, support the chairperson's efforts to keep the meeting to the point and within the time limits.

A chairperson should be someone who is accepted and respected by other members. Naturally, they should arrive on time and follow the administrative procedures correctly. They should also have done some preparation because they need to know enough to guide the discussion and to steer the meeting to a decision. The chairperson should introduce everyone and allow everyone to have their say while at the same time keeping the discussions to the point and controlling them so that no time is wasted. They should make sure that anything agreed is recorded and that procedures for follow-up are adhered to. At the end of the meeting, the chairperson sums up – the meeting should end on time.

Chairing a meeting is not an easy job but you should try to chair a meeting or two if you can. This will not only give you experience of the difficulties of keeping meetings short and relevant, it will also enable you to keep them from becoming time-wasting sessions.

Set time limits

If meetings drag on, then you are not setting time limits. These are vital to keep meetings on course. Everyone likes to have their say at meetings and a good chairperson will allow them to do so in turn. But some people repeat themselves and start straying from the point. Politely bring ramblers to an end. Announce at the start of the meeting how long you will be allowing for the meeting itself and for each person to speak. If people disagree, remind them how much their time is costing the company and that you would prefer it to be spent on more productive work rather than meetings.

Action, action

The main purpose of your meeting should be to suggest certain courses of action. One of the first jobs of a new meeting is to find out how many of these actions have been carried out. Use checklists to monitor progress. Do not confine this to the next meeting, send reminders to attendees between meetings to find out what progress has been made. Aim to ensure that the actions are carried out as far as possible before the next meeting.

Time and place

Choose the time and place for your meeting carefully. It is no good insisting that everyone turns up at a time when you know that they usually have other commitments. Holding meetings at unusual times, such as before normal work starting time when you know that people have to travel long distances, is going to leave you with members who are resentful, tired and disinclined to contribute in a meaningful way.

Choose a time when most of the people will be able to attend. Give plenty of warning so that either the time of the meeting can be changed if not enough people can attend, or people can make arrangements to be there.

Make sure that the place you choose is convenient too. If people have to travel to an inconvenient location you will find that attendance is low. Cold, uncomfortable meeting rooms are not suitable, either. If you have no choice about where you hold the meeting, at least try to ensure that it is warm and fresh. Try to make it as comfortable as possible and provide ample desk space. Also provide the basics – pens/pencils, spare paper, water and glasses, perhaps coffee/tea/soft drinks and refreshments.

Taking a break

Most people like a break in meetings, if only to go to the toilet or stretch their legs. Unless there is a pressing reason, one or two short breaks of a few minutes is all that is required. Refreshments can be taken during the discussion. A good chair will allow this but ensure that the break lasts only a few minutes. Longer breaks tend to become a social occasion and it gets more difficult to recall people to the table. As a participant don't abuse short breaks.

Any other business (AOB)

Any other business (AOB) is one of the most time-wasting parts of any meeting. You can race through the agenda with speed and efficiency only to find that AOB is used as an opportunity by members to speak about irrelevant subjects at length.

In most cases, AOB is entirely unnecessary. If the item was important it should have been submitted for the main agenda. Otherwise it can be dealt with by memo, phone calls, other staff or not at all. A good chairperson will disallow discussion on most AOB on these grounds.

If AOB is considered to be a necessary part of the meeting, it should not be put at the end of the agenda where it increases the danger of dragging the meeting out. It should be put at the beginning with only ten minutes allocated for it. That way there is a defined time limit, with the pressure of the main business of the meeting to follow to focus minds.

TIME MANAGEMENT TIP

Define *exactly* what kind of subjects, if any, can be raised under AOB.

Deal with interruptions

Meetings take much longer if they are constantly interrupted. The best way of handling interruptions is to deal with them as far as possible beforehand. Take these precautions:

- ask your secretary to deal with phone calls and callers
- deal with outstanding calls and visits beforehand
- warn potential visitors that you will be unavailable
- have strategies in place for emergencies so that your staff can deal with them.

If you are interrupted during the meeting, immediately direct the person to your secretary or a designated member of staff. Delegate one person at each meeting to deal with any interruptions.

————————— Feedback —————————

There is no point in holding meetings if you do not follow them up. When courses of action have been decided, follow them up to see whether they have been carried out.

Each meeting should result in a list of things to be done, and each individual should have the complete list with their responsibilities highlighted or initialled. Each action should be given a specific time limit. You should follow up these lists shortly after the meeting. Allow a few days for people to get started, then make a progress check. If they have not started or are struggling, find out where the problem lies – do they need more information? Someone to help them? Advice about where to start? Follow this up a few days later to make sure everything is on track.

The follow-up times can be adjusted according to the times set at the meeting. Make sure that everyone knows what other actions were agreed so they are aware of how they affect their own course of action.

Who will do what and when?

It is not enough to produce action lists. You need to make it clear who is going to do something and when it will be done by. If several people will be involved, make sure that they have arranged to get together to discuss their own share and to liaise. Check on this at regular intervals.

Monitoring progress of agreement

If the aim is to produce agreement by various parties, you must ensure that progress on this agreement is monitored. If there appear to be any problems these should be dealt with immediately so that progress is not held up.

—— Conferences and lectures ——

Strictly speaking, conferences and lectures are not meetings but the chance for people to obtain information and meet others in the same line of work. However, they can be as time wasting as meetings and you need to be aware of this.

Before you accept an invitation to any conference or lecture, decide whether it will be of use to you and other people. If only one or two speakers will be of interest, ask for copies of their speeches to be sent to you. If you have been asked to give a lecture but the situation will neither enhance your reputation or be useful enough for you to be present, offer a written copy for conference notes. If the conference has some potential use and interest but you are pressed for time, consider sending a member of your staff. Alternatively only attend one day of the conference.

Make the most of any conference you do attend by listening carefully to the talks that will be of most use. Make sure that you get a copy of the notes for the talk and take your own notes. If you socialise afterwards, take people's cards and write details about them on the back, together with any notes about their expertise and contact numbers. File these as soon as you return to your office.

— Review meetings' usefulness —

At regular intervals review the relevance of any meetings you go to – say at six monthly intervals. If the meeting is no longer useful or the items can usually be dealt with another way, do not attend any more. There will be some meetings that your boss will insist on you attending. These, of course, you must continue to go to unless you can persuade your boss that they should be less frequent. Other meetings can be dealt with by sending your staff. Now that you have reduced the number of meetings you go to, continue to review their usefulness and eliminate them when possible. That way you will only attend useful and well-run meetings and will save a great deal of time.

TOP TEN TIPS

1 Eliminate, avoid or delegate meetings.
2 Investigate other means of holding meetings.
3 Be clear about what you want any meeting to achieve.
4 Like anything else, a meeting should have a beginning, a middle and an end.
5 Take a turn at chairing a meeting, if possible.
6 Don't go to meetings if you have nothing to say.
7 Every meeting should result in action.
8 Action must be followed up.
9 Read the meeting papers beforehand.
10 Don't be late!

Summary

Meetings can be great time wasters. Many are irrelevant, time consuming or unnecessary. Do not attend any meetings that you do not have to – delegate, eliminate, and reduce. Meetings should have clear objectives and be well planned. A good chairperson and agenda will keep participants to the point. The meeting should have a starting and finishing time that is kept to. If you are not chairing the meeting support the chairperson's efforts to keep it on track. If possible, find other ways of holding meetings, such as by phone or video conferencing. Information can be provided in other ways than attending meetings.

10
THE ART OF
DELEGATING

This chapter explains how to get other people to do your work. It looks at how empowering your staff not only frees up your time but makes everyone more productive. By the end of the chapter you will feel confident about delegating work and choosing the right staff to do it.

Don't try to do it all

Are you one of those people who doesn't trust anyone else to do what needs to be done? Some people can't bear anyone else to help them in any way. They don't trust anyone to do a job as well as they can. It is not surprising that they then get overwhelmed by work and complain that they have far too much to do. It is their own fault. If they learnt to delegate they could have much more time available. You can learn to delegate and save much of your time.

Why delegate?

Delegating has advantages other than saving you time and freeing you to work on tasks that are important in your scheme of things and that will benefit the company more. If you delegate effectively, your staff will become more skilled and committed. This will contribute to the success of your team and section and the company as a whole. It will also show how good your managerial qualities are – a good point for promotion.

Effective delegation means that although decisions are taken lower down in the pecking order they are taken nearer to where the work is being done and problems occur. Your staff will often have a much better idea of what needs to be done than you do. That means that they can make decisions faster, and probably better. This, too, reinforces the successful image of you and your staff.

So, by delegating you can save time for more important work and improve the effectiveness and morale of your staff. So what's stopping you?

What happens if you don't delegate?

If you fail to delegate when possible and appropriate, you create a burden for yourself. Your staff will not have the authority, responsibility or information to make decisions themselves. They will lack confidence and become unable to take criticism. The result is that they will try to refer back to you whenever they can. That means you will be subjected to a string of interruptions. You are likely to respond by offering to deal with any problems just to stop the flow of staff to your door. But that means you will end up doing their work as well as yours. You will run out of time and your staff will run out of work. In the end it will be your staff who will be checking up on you to find out what progress has been made on work that they should have been doing.

Harriet, a conscientious middle manger in a clothing company, didn't believe in delegating work. She didn't trust anyone else to do it to her own exacting standards. Her staff became demoralised and resentful and her day was interrupted by her staff who constantly had to consult her about minor matters that they could have dealt with. It was not until a major contract was lost because Harriet failed to complete a project on time that she began to take delegation seriously.

This should be enough to convince you that delegating and empowering your staff is not only sensible but necessary if you are to do your own work well.

——— What is delegating? ———

Delegation is not telling your staff to do something and then hanging over them while they do it, or worrying constantly about how they are getting on. Delegation is giving your staff the authority and freedom to do a task you would normally do.

There are several levels of delegation. You can:

- delegate part of the job
- delegate the whole job
- delegate the work but expect to make all the major decisions
- delegate but expect frequent progress reports
- delegate and ask for the result at the end.

You can also delegate either authority or responsibility or both. You can give someone the authority to do something but be ultimately responsible for the result. Or you can make the person responsible but retain authority over how the work is carried out. Or you can delegate both authority and responsibility.

Ideally, you want to be able to delegate the authority needed to carry out the task so that the person doing the work can make the decisions about how it should best be done. A certain degree of responsibility should be delegated too – if the work is done badly then they should be told why and asked to put it right. But the ultimate responsibility for what your staff do always rests with you. It is your job to ensure that they produce the best work for you. They will do this if you delegate interesting and responsible tasks to them because they will appreciate the honour and rise to the challenge.

You will not, of course, delegate without ensuring that your staff are well prepared. But once you have delegated, you are free to get on with the work that you do best and for which you are paid.

TIME MANAGEMENT TIP

Ask your staff what *they* think they need to do a job well – and then supply it.

What to delegate

The jobs to delegate are those that are going to save you the most time. They are the things that your staff, or outside experts, can do better, quicker and cheaper than you can. Don't hand work out at random. Give staff work to do that will challenge and interest them and contribute to their training. You cannot provide interesting work all the time, of course, but you should try to delegate work that your staff will see as relevant to their own work and careers.

What not to delegate

You must not delegate tasks that are solely your responsibility and which you have been asked to carry out personally. You should not delegate overall leadership of your team nor final accountability for your team's work. The responsibility for choosing, training and appraising your subordinates is yours alone as is the task of promoting, praising and disciplining them (and, as said before, be generous with praise).

Empower your staff

Don't under-utilise your staff, however many of them there are. They are your most valuable time management tool. Given your confidence and proper training and preparation they can take much of your work from your shoulders. This does not mean overworking them but giving them more power to make their own decisions and to get on with work without being constantly checked by you.

Many staff feel undervalued and under-used. They do routine work competently but are not given a chance to prove their ability. The work they do becomes boring. By giving them more responsibility, you will be creating happier, more responsible staff who take a real interest in the work they do. You should be training all your staff to aim for the next grade up. The saying is that first-rate managers pick first-rate staff; second-rate managers pick third-rate staff. If you want to be the best, make sure that your staff are the best.

If your staff can eventually do your job, rejoice. They can deal with much of your work and train their replacement before they move onwards and upwards!

Whom to delegate to

In order to be effective, don't simply delegate to anybody who happens to be around. If you are to save time you need to delegate to someone whom you can trust to do the job well, with the minimum of monitoring, after proper preparation.

Find someone who you can trust and who has a similar attitude to the work as you do. Everybody has their own set of skills and experience, so pick someone who has attributes suitable for the task you want to delegate. Some of your staff will be specialists, so delegate tasks to them that make use of their special knowledge. You might also need to delegate work to your colleagues, or even your boss! If you are sure that they are the best people for the work, explain why you think their skills are needed and persuade them to do it.

Monica, a computer expert, had no hesitation in asking her boss, Philip, to contribute a section to her latest report. Philip had just won an industry award for a new technical innovation relevant to the report. Not only was he obviously the best person to write that section, he was flattered to be asked.

Don't, however, delegate work beyond someone's capabilities. There is a fine line between giving work of a sufficient level to be challenging, and work far beyond the person's abilities. Unless you match the work to a person's ability, they will become stressed because of their inability to do what is wanted at the standard required.

Outside experts

You might need to delegate some things to outside experts. Don't be afraid to do so if it will save time and be cost effective. However, outside specialists must justify their fees, so get a detailed breakdown of what they will do, when and for how much, before you start and ask for regular progress reports.

TIME MANAGEMENT TIP

When using outside experts, ask for breakdowns from three specialists. Remember that the cheapest will not necessarily be the best for the job.

Train for confidence

Before you let your staff get on with things you need to explain what you want of them. If you are giving them extra responsibilities you must explain why you are doing so and what is expected of them.

You will need to ensure that they know how to do whatever tasks you have in mind for them. Some things you will be able to explain yourself; others you must provide training for. This might be as simple as getting somebody more experienced to show them what to do, or it might mean providing training either outside or in-house to explain specialist techniques. However simple or complex the training needs are, you must make sure these are addressed first so that you can leave your staff to get on with the work you give them in confidence.

If you want them to make more decisions on their own account then they will need the information to do so. Make sure that they have this or that it is easily available. Explain to them what your criteria are for referring decisions to you or dealing with them themselves. They need to know what the perimeters of their responsibilities are.

Set clear boundaries on the work you delegate so that your staff know exactly how much responsibility and authority they have, and when and how you want to be involved. Encourage their independence but make it clear that you want certain standards to be achieved. Be consistent throughout the task about what you want done, and how and when.

When you delegate something, provide all the background information necessary so that there are no surprises when the work starts. Your staff need all the information about a project if they are to assume responsibility for it.

When to delegate

Delegate whenever you need to save time. If possible, delegate complete areas of responsibility to particular people so that they have complete command of certain aspects of the work.

Don't delegate at the last minute unless it is unavoidable. Allow plenty of time for training, advice and for getting to grips with what the work entails.

Don't just fling a whole project at someone either, until they are experienced enough to cope with it. Delegate small tasks first and build up or delegate work in stages. Don't rush a job; allow time for it to be understood and initiated. Later, with experience, the people you delegate to will be able to work much quicker when it is necessary.

You might think that it will take up too much of your time to train and advise people to do work that you have normally done. But the initial time spent on this is worth it because as your staff grow more confident and experienced, they will need less and less supervision.

Delegate phone calls

Start by delegating phone calls that your staff can deal with as well as you can. They should all have the phone call sheets and incoming call pads, as explained in Chapter 8. Encourage them to take full notes and if possible to deal with anything that arises themselves. Make clear what calls must come to you, for example, the boss, your mother, your bookmaker, and then expect them to deal with any other calls and only refer them to you if they cannot deal with them.

If particular problems arise frequently, one person could be delegated to deal with them or it could be done on a rota basis. If you do not have enough staff to allow for one person to be continually answering the phone, then everyone can take a turn for a set period during the week and free the rest of the staff to get on with their own work.

Let your staff solve the problems

Your staff are probably full of ideas about how particular problems can be solved. Let them tell you and then carry them out. You, of course, must bear the final responsibility but your staff should be able to deal with the day-to-day problems that occur themselves. In fact, the best people to solve problems are usually the people who are closest to them. So get your staff to solve as many problems as they feel capable of. As they get more confident they will solve more and more complex problems. Far from putting them off it will give them confidence.

Letters

Most of your staff should be able to deal with basic correspondence themselves. If you have given them permission to deal with as many problems as possible, then they should also be able to reply to them.

They should be encouraged to deal with the contents of the letter and respond accordingly, and be ready to deal with any follow-up results. That way less paperwork should reach you because it will have already been dealt with.

Standardise replies

You can help your staff by using standardised replies. Many calls and letters received will be on similar subjects. Ask your staff (and you should do the same) to make a list over a fortnight of the nature of calls and letters to them, for example, request for information, request to present sales pitch, enclosing information from the sales office. Make one master list and then work out a standard series of replies both for the phone and letters.

For phone replies, of course, you simply suggest the nature of the reply, for example, request for literature – say you'll send the latest catalogue. Letters are more complex but standard letters or standard paragraphs can be agreed. These can be amended slightly where necessary. Standard letters can be stored on the computers your staff use so they can be called up and amended as necessary. Or they can call up one or more standard paragraphs to insert into their letters.

Not all phone calls and replies can be dealt with like this but you will be surprised at how many can. By standardising you will substantially reduce both your own time and that of your staff. When you are dictating letters it is much quicker to say 'use standard letter number six and add such and such'.

Delegate major tasks where possible

You might think that I am advocating delegating just the routine and minor tasks. But major tasks can also be delegated. This requires a bit more effort on your part. Your staff must be adequately briefed and you must pay regular attention to them to encourage and help them. This does not mean that you should be constantly telling them what to do but that you will ask for regular progress reports and aim to know about problems before they escalate. Even this level of oversight will free up your time and enable you to concentrate your efforts elsewhere.

Don't just delegate the boring stuff

You might be tempted to delegate the boring and routine work, whether major or minor, on the grounds that you should be doing the interesting work. But if you never let your staff do any interesting work they will become bored and resentful. Nor will they progress enough to be able to help you with more complex issues.

By giving your staff as much interesting work as possible as well as routine work, you will truly empower them and they will feel part of your team. They will start to bring you ideas and you will all work together. When routine or boring work does have to be done they will be more likely to do it with good grace knowing that you are not deliberately keeping the interesting work for yourself.

——————— Don't do it for them ———————

You will lose the point of delegation if you insist on hanging over your staff and telling them what to do. You should prepare them as fully as possible beforehand and then let them get on with it. You will need regular progress reports and should be on hand if there are any problems, but on the whole you should leave them alone until the work is finished. The idea, after all, is for you to save time and get on with other things yourself. You can't do that if you are constantly trying to check up on your staff.

Also, if you keep looking over your staff's shoulders, they will lose confidence in themselves and think you don't trust them. Give people responsibility and show that you believe they can do the work and you will be pleasantly surprised at the result. Empowered staff feel valued and their productivity increases. They will find their own ways of saving time and effort which will rebound on you. So leave them to get on with it.

--------- **Help and resources** ---------

Your staff must be properly prepared for the work you want them to do. Make sure that all the necessary resources and help are available to them or that they can get them easily. Some of the things they might need are:

- equipment
- information
- assistants
- communications technology
- training
- advice
- standardised procedures
- someone to contact if problems occur.

It would be unfair to let them embark on work without providing them with all the help they might need. All this should be decided before they start so that deadlines aren't breached because of lack of resources or help. Help them by doing the following:

- agree the outcome
- delegate in good time
- give praise where it is due
- monitor and review progress
- evaluate
- make any changes together.

Agree the outcome

This might seem obvious but have you discussed with your staff exactly what you want from them when you give them a piece of work to do? Unless they know what you expect, they will be put in a position of possibly handing work in that is unsatisfactory because they didn't understand what was wanted.

You must also set clear deadlines for each stage of the task and its completion so that your staff can fit it in sensibly to their other work.

Explain carefully and fully what you expect to see both at the end of the task and at various stages during it.

Delegating has four stages:

1 Preparation.
2 Briefing.
3 Monitoring.
4 Reviewing.

Preparation

You must first prepare the ground on what you want done. You should know what it is that needs doing and have made sure that any help and resources needed will be readily available.

Briefing

You should make clear to your staff exactly what you want done and when. Also tell them how you want it done. Make sure they understand your instructions totally.

Monitoring

This is essential to ensure that everything is going as you wish and so that you can be on hand to solve any major problems that occur. But do not spend all your time overseeing a project – when possible let your staff get on with it. However, you will need to ask for regular progress reports, particularly on long projects.

Reviewing

Once the task has been completed, review it with the staff concerned. Ask what problems they had and what went well. Make suggestions and listen to theirs. By talking through the task on completion you can get an idea of the capabilities of your staff. Give praise where it is due!

Delegate in good time

If you want your staff to be able to do the work you give them, you must ensure that you delegate it in good time. It is unfair and dispiriting to give out work at the last minute and then expect staff to work under pressure to try to fit it in. It will not get done as well as you would like and your staff will naturally feel put upon and exploited.

Allow enough time for the task you give. Letters can be given at short notice, a project might need a week or more's notice if it is to be tackled properly.

Listen to your staff if they tell you that the time for preparation is too short. They, after all, are in the best position to know how much time they need to prepare for it. On the other hand, don't allow idlers to slow the work down.

TIME MANAGEMENT TIP

Allow time at the end of the job for checking and consolidation.

Praise where praise is due

I'm sure you've noticed that when someone praises your work you feel pleased and full of pride and attack your work with renewed vigour. Time seems to fly because you are high on praise. Do the same for your staff. Be generous with your praise when they do well. It is not only what they deserve, it will also inspire them. They will want to continue to do well and their productivity will increase.

On the other hand, don't hesitate to point out where something could have been done better. But do so in a positive manner so your staff feel that you are sharing the responsibility.

Derek, an editor, used to accept work without much comment. One day, feeling in a good mood, he praised a journalist who had done a competent but not startling piece of work. The result was amazing. The journalist suddenly felt recognised. His productivity improved as did the standard of his work. Derek saw that praise worked and began to be more generous with it. His staff responded to this with enthusiasm and the paper won a national award for excellence.

When you are dealing with inexperienced staff they will need more praise than usual to encourage them. But later, once they have had experience of the work, only give them praise for very good work.

Don't be afraid of praise. Be honest but generous with it and your staff will react positively.

Monitor and review progress

Whenever you delegate you must make sure that there are processes in hand for monitoring and reviewing progress. You might automatically get some feedback in the form of complaints or praise from clients. But generally, unless you take steps to monitor work, you will not know how it is going, perhaps until it is too late to correct any problems.

How much monitoring you do will depend on the experience of your staff and the amount of responsibility you have delegated to them.

Monitoring can be as simple as checking letters from your secretary at the end of each day until you are confident that they are capable of producing them without mistakes and with intelligent use of standard replies agreed beforehand. Normally, for longer projects, you will want to ask for regular written or spoken reports of progress. Sometimes the nature of the work will mean that you should hold regular staff meetings either *en bloc* or with individuals so that you can discuss progress.

You can check informally by asking staff how they are getting on, by inviting them to meet you for a brief chat, or by getting feedback from other team members or clients. Don't hang over them peering at what they are doing; if you need to keep an eye on them, cast a casual look as you go about your ordinary business. More formally, you can ask to see what is produced, such as reports or letters, or by collecting and analysing statistical data. On important jobs you might want regular formal progress reports, whether written or oral, and a full report on completion.

At the end of any project you should review it with the staff concerned, so that you can praise good points and discuss where things could have been improved. Making a written record of this and agreeing new ways of working means that next time efficiency is increased and problems are reduced. Do not ignore this important part of delegation. It will only take a small part of your time and will pay dividends in terms of improved ways of working.

Evaluation

You must take time to evaluate any delegated work. This is so that you can tell whether you have delegated the right kind of work to the right members of staff and that it has been done to the standards required and on time.

Ask yourself whether the objectives have been met and whether it was completed within its budget. Be honest with yourself about the quality and quantity of support that you gave. Was it appropriate and adequate? Were any problems dealt with correctly? And how effective was the monitoring process?

By taking some time to evaluate delegated tasks, you will save time by delegating more effectively next time.

Make changes together

Do not make changes arbitrarily without discussing them with your staff. You will have agreed processes beforehand so that your staff can be left to get on with the work. But sometimes you will have to ask them to make changes in the work itself or in the way it is done, or your staff may come across problems that necessitate changes.

Whatever the reason for changes, they should be discussed with your staff and not simply imposed upon them. Your staff should understand what they are being asked to change and why. By discussing them together you are making it clear that you are agreeing to and are involved in the changes and that you are supportive of them.

Talk through any changes as soon as it becomes clear that they need to be made. You might need to decide:

- whether a deadline needs to be changed
- if a new way of working is appropriate
- if new equipment is necessary
- whether some extra training or support is required.

Do not make changes for the sake of it. Your staff may have other solutions to the problems and it is important to hear their comments and suggestions before imposing any changes.

Empowerment produces efficiency

Empowering your staff does not reduce your status or worth in the organisation. What it does is to give confidence and a sense of worth and purpose to your staff. It also frees time for you to get on with more important work. Your time should be spent on the goals and activities that are important to you in the workplace and at home. Empowering your staff allows you to concentrate on these. It also improves efficiency within the company so that not only you but the entire organisation benefits.

Don't be delegated to

You have now saved considerable amounts of your time by delegating work to others. But suppose you get a lot of work delegated to you. How can you cut down on that?

First of all, only accept if it is consistent with your own goals. As you are likely to get work delegated by your boss, refer to Chapter 6 on ways of saying 'no'. When you do have to accept work, don't accept blindly. Make sure you understand what is required of you and that clear objectives and standards have been set.

Ask for any information, help and advice that you need. At the end of the work, ask for feedback so that you can evaluate your own performance.

TOP TEN TIPS

1 Choose the right person.
2 Delegate now.
3 Allow enough time for completion.
4 State objectives clearly.
5 Provide all the information.
6 Ensure all staff understand the task.
7 Set deadlines.
8 Monitor progress regularly.
9 Be available for clarification and advice.
10 Take responsibility, but praise the person doing the work.

Summary

Don't be afraid to delegate – it will not undermine your authority but will free time for you to do what you do best. Delegate recurring tasks and tasks that others can do better, quicker and cheaper than you. Match the work to the person and don't just delegate the boring and routine work. Time taken to train, monitor and evaluate delegated work and staff is saved by being able to delegate a similar task the next time it occurs. Letters and phone calls can be delegated and suitable standard replies prepared. You should aim to delegate as much as possible but not to accept much delegated work yourself.

11

DEAL WITH INFORMATION OVERLOAD

This chapter helps you to deal with the astonishing amount of information that we receive nowadays. By learning techniques to deal with it you can free a lot of time.

—— Where does it all come from? ——

To keep up with work, hobbies, finances and all the other parts of your life you need information. But we all receive far more than we can ever usefully absorb or use. Some information is obviously important. But everybody is subjected to such a vast amount. Think about where it can come from:

- junk mail
- books
- magazines
- newsletters
- radio
- TV
- advertisements
- e-mail
- faxes
- letters
- catalogues.

It is tempting to regard all information as equally important and to try to absorb as much of it as possible. But life is too short to do that. You need to work out what you need to know, how to absorb it effectively and how to deal with unwanted information.

TIME MANAGEMENT TIP

Keep an account of all the different ways you receive information in a typical week. Add up the amount of time it takes you to read/listen/watch it. Now you see why reducing information overload is so important!

—— What do you need to know? ——

You need to work out what the minimum is that you need to know in order to deal with or understand the parts of your life. If you want a particular phone number, for example, you don't read the whole phone directory, you look up the one you want. In the same way, whatever information you need usually has a minimum requirement. Anything above that should be for interest or leisure and fitted into your leisure time. For example, you only need one trade magazine or newsletter to keep up with industry information, not six or seven.

Cost

There is a cost in money as well as time from getting too much information. Magazines and books cost money; specialist newsletters are particularly expensive. Time taken to absorb unnecessary information is a waste of your salary – reading two unnecessary magazines could waste an hour's worth of your time and the company's money.

TIME MANAGEMENT TIP

Work out what an hour of your time is worth according to your salary. Before you decide to read or watch something, ask yourself whether it is really worth the cost to you and your company.

—— Eliminate reading material ——

What do you have to read during the course of a week? Perhaps it includes the following:

- newspapers
- magazines
- books
- reports
- e-mail
- letters.

Some of these will be directly related to your work; others will be for pleasure only; some will be related to both your work and home life.

Trying to read all of this can take over your life. A lot of the work that people take home is reading that they simply haven't been able to catch up on during working hours. Think of the time you could save by simply eliminating much of your reading material!

You must not, of course, eliminate anything that you have to read, simply everything that you don't need to read.

Your first task is to cancel any reading material sent to you that you feel is unnecessary. If you are on the reading list for magazines and newsletters sent in-house, go through the list carefully and ask for your name to be taken off all but the most essential of them. You might need one magazine related to your work; not ten. If you personally subscribe to magazines, decide whether they are all really necessary. If not, cancel your sub now. You will have more reading time and more money.

Junk mail can be eliminated by contacting the Mail Preference Service (see Useful Addresses) and unsolicited phone calls can be reduced by contacting the Telephone Preference Scheme (see Useful Addresses).

Don't fill in coupons asking for brochures or information – your name will go onto the mailing lists. Don't buy or borrow books that you will have no time to read. (When you have read this chapter, however, you will have enough saved time to read for pleasure.) If you need books, borrow them from the library or company archive rather than buying them, otherwise you will be paying unnecessary costs.

You probably automatically receive reports from your company. Don't ask for minutes, reports or any other documentation just for the sake of it. Eliminate the reading matter that every workplace creates by taking your name off automatic internal mailing lists.

How to reduce the bulk

Sometimes the sheer bulk of reading matter can be off-putting. But you can reduce this by judicious use of tearing and copying. When you receive one of your, now few, magazines, check through it quickly to see if any articles are of interest. Then tear them out, or get your secretary to photocopy them for reading later. Tear out newspaper articles (if it's your paper) or get them copied. Once your secretary knows what you are looking for they can mark articles and chapters for you beforehand.

Press cuttings

For many people, keeping up with the latest news about their company, product or profession is an important part of their job. However, this can mean reading through several newspapers every day.

You can deal with this by using a press cuttings service. For a monthly fee, a cuttings agency will send you clippings of articles with any mention of the subject, individual or company that you specify. This will usually include relevant magazines, too. Individual agencies will specify what print media they cover.

At regular intervals, usually weekly, you will be sent a batch of cuttings on the subject you specified. Try to define the subject as specifically as possible. Alan, a vet, was writing a book about Persian cats. He asked his secretary to write to a cuttings agency to arrange cuttings on that subject for the next six months. Unfortunately his secretary, distracted by a phone call, only typed the word 'cats' into the letter. For weeks afterwards, Alan received a cutting of every article that included any mention of the word 'cat' – cat suits, Sea Cat, big cats, cat flap, etc. Trying to find mention of Persian cats in the resulting mass of paper was hopeless. By the time the mistake was rectified, Alan had spent money and time on irrelevant information.

You can find a list of press cuttings agencies in *Willings Press Guide* or *The Writer's Handbook*, both of which should be in your local library.

Newsletters

Newsletters are a temptation, too. They always claim that you cannot do without them. That may be partially true, but one is usually more than adequate for keeping up to date with what is going on in your line of business. Take your name off the subscription list of any newsletter not vital to you and use the tear and copy technique again.

Computer printout

Companies produce vast amounts of computer printed paper. Do not get into the habit of accepting it all. Ask to be sent only computer printouts that are directly relevant and important for your work. Get your staff to screen all computer-generated paper that comes into the office and to eliminate anything irrelevant or unnecessary. Get taken off distribution lists for computer-generated documents.

Catalogues

Catalogues are another common source of information overload. Many companies and individuals receive dozens of them. Managers often find them useful for keeping abreast of the latest products in their line of business and for seeing what their rivals are up to. But you can get inundated with them.

Ask to be taken off the mailing lists of any company whose catalogues you never look at. Limit yourself to the most important or relevant catalogues. Skim them quickly, make a note of anything useful, and then throw them away. If you do need to keep them, keep only the up-to-date issues. Likewise, your secretary should limit their intake of office supplies catalogues. Skim catalogues from new firms – if they are not useful, get taken off their list.

Eric runs a small building firm and generally receives a lot of catalogues. He hadn't realised how many until a paper recycling effort during the three months before Christmas. He collected two large cardboard boxes of catalogues that arrived by post during that period –

this was in addition to the catalogues he had lying around. Not only were there more than he could sensibly look at, they also took up a lot of space. Now he has arranged to receive catalogues only from the few firms he usually does business with. He lets his secretary judge whether new firms' catalogues are worth seeing.

——— Reading in transition time ———

What do you do with the reduced pile of articles and papers that you need to read at some point? This is where the transition time talked about in Chapter 4 comes into play. Put all your reading material into one folder. Whenever you get a few spare minutes, take out one of the papers and read it. You can then file it (rarely) or throw it away.

Take your reading folder when you travel by public transport or know that you will have a few minutes' waiting time during the day. Try not to take any home.

——— How to read effectively ———

Anybody can improve their reading technique by following a few simple rules. Use these methodically for everything you have to read (except when you read for pleasure) and you will drastically reduce the amount of time you spend on reading, while still absorbing the necessary information.

Books

1 Read the chapter list to get an idea of the content.
2 Scan the index to see what is covered and in how much detail.
3 Read the introduction.
4 Read the introduction to any relevant chapters and the last page.
5 Read the chapter quickly.
6 Reread any important parts of the chapter.

If you are reading an information book, you rarely need to read it all. By following the above procedure you can reduce the amount of time it takes to get to the relevant information.

Documents and articles

Documents and articles can be read in a similar way.

1 Read the abstract/précis/introduction (in the case of academic or professional documents or articles) or the first few paragraphs to gauge content.
2 Read the conclusion or final few paragraphs. In many cases, or if you are short of time, that will be all you need to read. If you need to absorb it in more detail then:
3 Read the relevant sections.

This might seem obvious but it is surprising how many people who should know better start at the beginning of any reading material and read it doggedly to the end, whatever its importance or relevance. If you take most reading material in the way suggested above, you can quickly gauge its importance. You can then easily pick out the parts that really do warrant being read all the way through.

There are five kinds of reading:

1 Reading for detailed study, for example, reading a legal document.
2 Slow reading, for example, novels.
3 Preview reading to get the gist quickly (as explained in previous paragraphs).
4 Skimming to get a general overview.
5 Rapid reading.

The first two are obvious and you are already capable of doing them. The third, previewing and quickly digesting the overall sense, we have discussed above.

The next kind of reading is skimming. This involves reading across and down the pages as you normally do but not taking in all of the words. Reading like this enables you to read faster but at the same time to absorb the general sense of what is being said. It enables you quickly to pick out the relevant part of the text for rereading in more detail. With practise you can learn to skim very quickly. It is a useful skill.

Speed reading

The last kind of reading is rapid reading or 'speed' reading and this is the kind that is usually taught by speed-reading courses. In Chapter 4

I pointed out that speed reading was not necessary but that some people find it helpful. I suspect that most people simply cannot, or do not want to spend the time needed to practise and consolidate such a skill. The techniques outlined above will be enough for them. But people who have persevered with learning speed reading say that they find it useful.

In the Western world we read from left to right and top to bottom. If we read reasonably quickly we take in phrases rather than one word at a time. Our eyes scan across the page, as in the skimming described above. To improve our reading speed we need to read down the centre of the page, reading words in batches rather than singly, and taking in words on either side.

By casting your eyes down the centre of the page you can get the sense quickly and need only look to the left or right if you spot something you need to pay more attention to. This method relies on the fact that we are capable of seeing and taking in the sense of groups of words. You can practise recognising which words or groups of words you can safely ignore.

You can use your finger or a pointer to guide your eyes along the text and this too helps speed up your reading. You can test how well you absorb information by reading a page of text as fast as possible and then seeing how much you can remember from it.

If you want to study rapid reading in more detail, refer to courses mentioned in Useful Addresses but you can achieve a faster reading speed on your own simply by practising these simple methods regularly.

Taking notes

Don't be afraid to take notes while you read. You might think this is wasting time and will slow you up. But it will consolidate what you have read. The information will stick in your mind better and eliminate the need to go back and reread something several times because you haven't taken it in or understood it.

Use your pen or a highlighter to mark relevant passages or underline important words and phrases as you go along. If you need to keep the reading material, you will easily be able to find the relevant items that are marked. If you will be throwing it away, it will still help to impress the information on your mind.

Rebecca, an up-and-coming finance officer with a local council, used to get mocked by her colleagues for taking notes while reading. They thought it was a waste of time to make notes about material already written down. Rebecca had the last laugh – she was the only person who understood a particularly lengthy written proposal well enough to argue against it at a full council meeting. She had absorbed the facts effectively by taking notes, and used them to jog her memory.

Reducing TV and radio

Reading is probably the main cause of information overload but there are other causes that you can deal with.

One obvious cause is the radio and TV. If you have these on a lot, you are wasting time and also receiving much information that is useless or irrelevant.

The answer is to turn them off. There will be some programmes that you particularly want or need to watch or listen to but you can find out what these are beforehand and only turn your TV or radio on when the time is right.

If a programme is particularly important to you, perhaps an Open University programme, use a video or tape recorder to record the programme for viewing or listening to at a convenient time. This is particularly useful for programmes at unsociable times of the night.

Do not, however, do what some people do and record lots of programmes and never listen to or watch them. If you only record the really relevant ones you can timetable a viewing half hour or hour into your day or week. Otherwise, you will simply get a backlog of recordings that you will never have time to watch.

Eric, an engineer, used to video his favourite TV programmes during the week and look forward to viewing them on Friday evenings. But he accumulated so many recordings that even several nights' viewing failed to reduce the heap significantly. Now he limits himself to one long-playing tape and videos no more than one or two programmes a week. If he doesn't get around to viewing them on Friday evening, he records over them. That way he does not get depressed by a pile of unseen tapes.

Computer information

A great deal of information now reaches us through computers. If you have access to e-mail and the Internet you can not only search for information yourself but a lot of information will be downloaded onto your computer each time you log in.

E-mail

The e-mail system is now so popular that people can find that they have hundreds of messages to deal with every day. If you have tagged your e-mail by different categories or given yourself different e-mail names for various contacts, you should find it sorted for you. You can read any relevant mail and ignore the rest.

If your system allows it, you can set up a different mail box for each subject or name you use. You need read only the e-mail in the relevant boxes and can either skim or delete mail in other mailboxes.

It is useful to set up a mail box that collects any e-mail with '£' or '$' signs, or the word 'money' in its title. These e-mails are likely to be junk mail and can all be deleted unread. Likewise, you can set up useful mail boxes to collect personal mail (under your name), and boxes for each of your areas of work or company sections. So, for example, you might have a mail box to collect all mail from the finance department or health and safety sections. You can also set up mail boxes for mail from particular people, such as your boss. By giving careful thought to what mail boxes you set up, you can reduce the amount of e-mail you have to deal with and make dealing with relevant e-mail much easier.

TIME MANAGEMENT TIP

Give your e-mail boxes specific rather than general names. Make sure that they are different enough not to confuse you.

You can also sort the mail in each mailbox into separate files. This means that you can call up all the mail on a certain subject, or by the sender of the e-mail, or by any other category you have chosen. So, for example, within a mailbox labelled 'training' you might sort mail into files for in-house training, personal training, and outside training.

You could have mailboxes and/or folders for:

- action items
- reference items
- key areas of your responsibility
- a group of similar functions
- 'bring forward' items.

By separating your e-mail into labelled files and mailboxes, you can prioritise it and read and reply to it as necessary. It should no longer be necessary to deal with it all in one go.

News groups

These are another main source of information overload. If you subscribe to one or more news groups via your e-mail and Internet connection, you will receive hundreds of articles downloaded onto your computer each time you log on.

There is no way you can read them all. However, there may be some of interest. Set up your e-mail system so that only the subject heading, not the whole article, is downloaded. That way you can choose which articles you want to read in full and download them as necessary. The rest can be deleted. Unless you do this regularly, you will find that your computer is clogged with unwanted news.

Listening

You might think that listening has nothing to do with reading or too much information. But listening effectively can reduce the need to ask for information to be written down for reading again later, unless it is vital for legal purposes.

Listening effectively can save time by:

- reducing the need for repetition
- eliminating the need for clarification
- keeping conversations short and relevant
- eliminating written explanations
- reducing the need for further conversations.

Listening is a skill and very few people do it well. You need to concentrate on what the other person is saying and remember the important points. At the same time, you need to convey to the speaker that you are paying attention to what they are saying and that you are taking it seriously.

Do not be embarrassed about taking brief notes while someone is talking to you. This will reinforce what they are saying. However, if you think that you or they would find it inhibiting, write notes immediately afterwards while the conversation is fresh in your mind.

Improve your listening skills by:

- asking pertinent questions
- asking for clarification if necessary
- showing that you are listening
- looking at the speaker
- being genuinely interested.

TOP TEN TIPS

1 Take your name off mailing lists for newsletters, catalogues, etc.
2 Learn to read for information – not in full.
3 Eliminate junk mail and junk phone calls.
4 Only record programmes you will have time to watch or listen to.
5 Don't subscribe to more than one or two news groups – delete most articles unread.
6 Learn to listen effectively – it saves time later.
7 Take notes while reading or listening.
8 Only look for information you actually need now.
9 Tear articles from magazines.
10 You don't need to know everything – only where to find it.

Summary

You do not need all the information that you are bombarded with every day. Screen out unimportant and irrelevant paper and ask for your name to be removed from unnecessary distribution lists both within and outside the company. Reduce the reading material you have to essentials and keep a special file for reading during spare time. Practise previewing material and take speed-reading lessons if you want to read much faster. Do not listen to or watch TV or radio programmes indiscriminately. Control e-mail by arranging for junk e-mail to be filed in a special mailbox. You can then delete it without reading it.

12
TIME MANAGEMENT TRAINING

This chapter explains how to introduce your staff to the benefits of time management techniques. It describes the types of training available and explains where to start with in-company training.

— Bring your expertise to work —

You have read this book, you've put the ideas into practice and the results have been good. Have you put these into practice at work or confined them to your home life 'just to see if they work'? If you haven't put the ideas into practice at work, do so now. Tell your staff what you are doing. Enlist the help of your secretary. Encourage your staff to try some of the techniques, too. Together you will start to make a difference.

— Why tell your staff? —

Common sense should tell you that it is no good to save time yourself if people around you are continuing in the same old way. If, for example, you are dealing with paper in the ways suggested but your staff are still working in a mess under piles of paper, or you turn up for meetings well prepared but nobody else has read the necessary papers, your time saving and efficiency will go no further than your desk before it gets bogged down in others' inefficiency.

Nigel headed a large sales section in a large company. He had read many books on time management and had attended a training course on the subject in his own time. His desk was uncluttered, he planned his days carefully and tried to make good use of every moment. Unfortunately, he had not asked his staff to work the same way. Whenever he thought he had got his paperwork sorted and settled down to work, his staff sent him unnecessary memos and kept popping in to ask him questions. His carefully planned days were disrupted. In frustration, he invited a time management expert to talk to his staff. Half way through the talk one of his staff turned to him and said 'So, that's what you were up to!' It turned out that his staff had regarded his changed habits as a personal quirk. Once they realised the benefits of what he was doing and how it applied to them, too, they were enthusiastic and the efficiency of the section increased rapidly.

If you want your life to run as smoothly as possible, you must train others in your ways. The more people who use time management techniques, the more you will save time in your own life and become less stressful.

People often work in a particular way only because they have not been shown any other way of doing it. If you take the time to explain your techniques to them, you can take all the benefit.

TIME MANAGEMENT TIP

Start by showing a few key staff how you want them to work – if you enthuse them, others will follow.

— Do they know what you want? —

It is no good bounding into the office on Monday morning and announcing 'From now on I want everyone to be efficient and save time. Start using time management techniques now.' Some people may understand what you mean but others will not have a clue.

Unless you explain to your staff exactly what you want them to do, you will get a hotchpotch of systems and be no better off.

It is important to get all your staff involved because some time management techniques can be applied throughout the office or company. For example, if everyone uses the same filing system then anyone in the company can quickly get hold of information. If everyone uses a different system in a company where people often change rooms and jobs, time will be wasted while a new filing system is learnt.

—— What training can you get? ——

The best person to train your staff in time management techniques is yourself. If you can spare the time to explain your way of working and the time management techniques that you find effective, then do so.

However, if you do not have the time (even when you have followed all my advice) there are other ways of learning about time management and individuals and organisations who can help you. Some of these are listed in Useful Addresses and Further Reading. The main training avenues open to you are:

- audio tapes
- videos
- TV
- books
- individual instructors
- management training organisations
- watching other people.

Audio tapes and videos

Many individuals and organisations have brought out their own time management tapes and videos. Ask in your local library or look in the small ads in business magazines.

TV

There are now many management and business programmes broadcast on TV. Some of these are relevant to time management. These kinds of programmes tend to be broadcast late at night or in the early hours of the morning, so you might need to video them for watching later. Check the TV listings in your newspaper or magazine.

Books

Books (like this one) can also help. Reading this book should enable you to rework your life drastically and save time. Other books can give ideas that you can adapt and add to the ones you have learnt here (see Further Reading.) Be like Barry, who was keen to learn time management techniques and applied it to his reading. He borrowed a time management book and read a chapter a day in one of his ten minute transition times.

Individual instructors

Some outside experts arrange seminars in which they explain and inspire people with their ways of working. Others will arrange to come into the workplace and train people there. Yet others will guide individuals through their working day, helping and encouraging them to use time management techniques. Some time management experts undertake a time management audit first; others will simply explain their techniques and leave it to you to implement them.

Management training organisations

There are now many organisations that run either management training courses with time management sections or specific time management courses. One example is the Institute of Management, which runs workshops and seminars on a wide range of management topics. Its short, non-accredited courses are open to everyone, not just IM members. Your company might pay the fees if you can persuade it that a course will be useful. Many IM courses are relevant to the ideas discussed in this book. One in particular is the Introduction to Management which includes modules on Self and Task Management and Managing People, as well as others. Contact the non-accredited programmes department for a short course brochure.

Individuals and organisations that provide training in time management techniques usually offer courses lasting one or two days. If you are paying for an individual to give you intensive personal instruction that might last for a long period, you will be seen at regular intervals over a period of time. Of course, you will have to pay for this.

Watching other people

One of the best ways of picking up useful time management tips is to watch how other people do it. There are probably one or two people you know who always seem to have a great deal to do and yet who are organised and happy and always have time for friends, family and outside interests.

Don't be shy. Ask them how they do it. What techniques do they use? Watch how they cope with stressful and busy times. Do they use any specific time management tools or do they have their own? Try out their ideas and techniques. Don't feel you have to adopt them all. Choose the ones that work best for you.

Whatever kind of training you choose, allow time for reviewing and consolidating what has been taught and for adapting these to your own working environment.

———— Ask your staff ————

Do not forget to ask your staff for their own time-saving ideas. Often, they will have a better way of doing something or can suggest something that the rest of your staff can adapt.

It may be that when you tell them your ideas, one or more will say 'Yes, but if you do this or that it will be even quicker/more efficient/more effective'. This is just the kind of response you want. You not only want people to do what you advise as far as time management is concerned, but also to bring their own experience to the situation. As the people in the front line, they will know the best way of doing things and you should introduce these ideas into the scheme as far as is practicable.

No time management scheme is set in stone. There are always other or better ways of doing things. Let your staff tell you what they are and act on them. Techniques will also vary between organisations and individuals. It is up to you to decide which ones are most useful to you and your staff.

Organising training

You or your company should organise specific time management training. Either bring in an outside firm or arrange to do the training yourself with the help of others within the company. However you do it, make sure that all the staff are informed and you arrange it for a time that they can all be there. You should attend, too, not only to see if there are techniques you can add to your repertoire but also to find out what your staff will be taught.

Arrange a training day or even a training week when time management techniques are learnt and put into practice. You might want to organise separate days for specific training in time-saving phone techniques or how to run meetings, for example.

Form a committee to oversee time management training and to follow up. Elect co-ordinators who will motivate other staff and spread information about the training and techniques throughout the company. Make sure that the training is widely publicised. If necessary, provide a compulsory training day or half day for each section of the company.

Give everyone a copy of a time management book (why not this one?) so that they have the basics to hand and can study and absorb them at leisure.

Briefing your staff

Unless you are introducing a personal time management expert to take each individual through a personal time audit, you should brief your staff in groups. This has the advantage of allowing your staff to put forward ideas that could be of benefit to everyone and offer further opportunities to discuss them.

Aim for co-operation rather than dictatorship. You are more likely to get co-operation if you can show that you are making an effort to introduce these techniques into your own working practices.

The first task – clear all desks

As your first task, find a new way of dealing with paper. This involves clearing everyone's desk and following the advice in Chapter 7. Once all the paper has been sorted out and everyone's desk is clear of clutter, introduce time-planning techniques and the use of diaries, lists and planners as described in Chapter 3.

TIME MANAGEMENT TIP

Ask the most efficient person on your staff to clear their desk first, then help others.

One step at a time

You will get disheartened if you expect everyone to manage their time perfectly immediately. Nobody is suddenly going to turn into a paragon of efficiency overnight. Introduce one time management technique at a time. So, for example, you could spend one day reorganising the filing system. Once people have got used to that, you could introduce techniques for dealing with interruptions ... and so on. By introducing one thing at a time and making sure that everyone understands how it works, your staff are more likely to get into good habits and continue with it.

Allow time

Introducing time management to your staff can backfire if you don't allow enough time for the practices to become part of everyday habits. If you are too impatient, people will become disheartened because they are still in the throes of discovering the best ways of getting things done. Give everyone time to get used to the changes. There are bound to be mistakes at first and sometimes it will seem as if it will never work. But gradually it will all come together and you will all reap the benefits.

Allow time for each step to be consolidated. Don't pile on too much at once. It might take as long as six months to get a system fully operational and ingrained into people's ways of working. But once it has done, efficiency will increase enormously.

Encouragement

Introducing time management will go down better if you give it your personal encouragement. You should be seen to be putting into practice the ideas that you have advocated for your staff. You should be encouraging everyone to practise time management techniques. After all, if you don't like doing it, nobody else will.

Once your staff see that it does make a difference, they will be enthusiastic and will start to bring their own ideas to the situation.

Monitoring

You should monitor what progress is being made. Walking about and seeing for yourself is probably the best way. Or delegate someone to do so (in a friendly fashion) and report back.

If certain techniques do not seem to be working, ask yourself why. Is it because:

- you haven't explained them properly?
- your staff haven't understood?
- more training is needed?
- the staff are not suitable for the situation?

Take a look at what you need to do to improve matters. It could be that some slight adjustments will make the scheme workable.

Review and consolidation

After a suitable period, say six weeks, you should review the situation to see what is working and what isn't. Did it start well but some people are now slacking? Are some schemes unworkable? Do the staff dislike some aspects of the plan? Now is the time to sort these out. Review it again after six months to find out how the system is progressing.

——— Keep up the good work ———

To make sure that staff remain motivated once the new system has been introduced and that they do not lapse into their old time-wasting ways, arrange for regular follow-up sessions. These could be monthly, quarterly or yearly and will set ongoing goals for time management within the workplace. The committee should meet regularly, too. At these follow-up sessions, encourage brainstorming for new ideas to save time and become more efficient. Turn it into a competition. Persuade the company to offer a yearly or six-monthly prize for the time management technique that saves the company the most time and/or the most money.

What next?

Now you have finished this book you will have started to introduce your own time management ideas. You will be working more efficiently and effectively and still get everything done with time to spare. Set an example to your staff so that they can see what the benefits are. Let your staff know which methods you prefer and the way you prefer them to operate.

With your good example, and your staff's co-operation, you will soon be running the most efficient organisation in the country!

TOP TEN TIPS

1 Set a good example – use time management techniques yourself.
2 Listen to your staff's ideas.
3 Choose the method of training that suits you.
4 If using an outside expert, ask to talk to a company that has used their services.
5 Arrange one or more time management training days.
6 Train all your staff, and ideally the whole company.
7 Make the first task to clear all desks.
8 Monitor and review the training.
9 Train by encouragement and example.
10 Build time management consolidation into the company.

———————— **Summary** ————————

You can practise time management techniques on your own but you will be more effective if you can get your staff to follow suit. There are many methods for teaching time management but the best person to introduce them into your workplace is yourself. You might think it worthwhile to bring in outside experts to arrange specific training days.

Introduce time management a bit at a time. Arrange for half-day or day sessions throughout the company and create a committee to spread information and follow up. Introduce one step at a time and evaluate progress regularly. Hold regular review sessions to motivate staff and encourage new ideas.

FURTHER READING

Adair, John *Effective Time Management*, Pan, 1982

Atkinson, Jacqueline *Better Time Management*, Thorsons, 1992

Black, Roger *Getting Things Done*, Michael Joseph, 1987

Bracey, Ronald *Maximise Your Time*, David Grant, 1997

Eisenberg, Ronni *Organise Yourself*, Piatkus, 1986

Forsyth, Patrick *First Things First*, Pitman, 1994

Gleeson, Kerry *The Personal Efficiency Program*, John Wiley & Sons, 1994

Godefroy, Christian H and John Clark, *The Complete Time Management System*, Piatkus, 1989

Hopson, E and Scally, M *Time Management – Conquering the Clock*, Mercury, 1991

Johns, Ted *Perfect Time Management*, Arrow, 1993

Levy, Mike *Get Yourself Organised!*, David Grant, 1997

Lockwood, Goergene *The Complete Idiot's Guide to Organising Your Life*, Alpha Books, 1996

Mayer, Jeffrey J *Time Management For Dummies*, IDG Books, 1995

Pollar, Odette *Get Organised!*, Kogan Page, 1993

Robertson, Arthur K & William Proctor *Work A 4 Hour Day*, William Morrow, 1994

Scott, Martin *Time Management*, Century, 1992

Smith, Jane *How To Be a Better Time Manager*, Kogan Page, 1997

Treacey, Declan *Clear Your Desk!*, Century, 1991

Treacey, Declan *Successful Time Management in a week*, Headway, 1993

Willings Press Guide, Hollis Directories Ltd, annually

Winston, Stephanie, *The Organised Executive*, Kogan Page, 1994

Woodhull, Angela V *The New Time Manager*, Gower, 1997

Turner, Barry *The Writer's Handbook*, Macmillan, annually

USEFUL ADDRESSES

UK

DAY-TIMERS Europe Limited
FREEPOST ANG6275
Hertford
SG13 7YE
Freephone 0800-854806
Fax: 0990-143580
(Planner/diary system)

Filofax UK
Unit 3, Victoria Gardens
Burgess Hill
West Sussex
RH15 9NB
Tel:01444-238 100
(Planner/diary system)

Institute of Management
3rd Floor, 2 Savoy Court
Strand
London
WC2R 0EZ
Tel: 0171-497 0580
Fax: 0171-497 0463

Institute of Management Foundation
Management House
Cottingham Road
Corby
Northants
NN17 1TT
Tel: 01536-204222 (Ask for the non-accredited programmes department)
Fax: 01536-201651
E-mail:institute@easynet.co.uk
(Management training)

Maximizer
JI Software
Graham Lloyd Building
Ampthill Road
Bedford
MK42 9JJ
Tel: 01234-214004
Fax: 01234-215374
Internet:http://www.maximizer.
   co.uk
(Management database system for Windows)

Mail Preference Service
FREEPOST 22
London
W1E 7EZ

Telephone Preference Scheme
Tel: 0800-398 893

Spearhead Training
Spearhead Training Group Ltd
Thorpe Close
Thorpe Way Trading Estate
Banbury
Oxfordshire
OX16 8SW
Tel: 01438-82115 or
Fax: 01438-821182 (brochure)
Tel: 01295-250010 (information and booking)
Fax: 01295-268382 (booking)
(Non-residential management training courses)

Australia

Ray Prince Associates
Brisbane
Australia
E-mail: rprince@ozemail.com.au
(Management consultants)

Realtime Time Management Pty Ltd
2/29 Madison Avenue
Narre Warren
VIC Australia
Tel: +613-9796 0777
Fax: +613-9796 0888
E-mail: info@tm.com.au

USA

Aun & Associates
2901 E Irlo Bronson Memorial Highway
The Aun Plaza, Suite D
Kissimmee
Florida 34744-5600
USA
Tel: (407) 870 0030
Fax: (407) 870 2088
E-mail: aunline@msn.com
(Speaker and seminar leader, including time management)

Franklin Covey Co
2200 W Parkway Blvd
Salt Lake City
UT 84119 2331
USA
Tel: 801-975 1776
Fax: 801-977 1431
(Time management day-planner)

The Productivity Institute
60 Huntingdon Street
PO Box 2126
Huntingdon
CT 06484
USA
E-mail: ctsm@aol.com
(Seminars)

Thomas Group, Inc
5215 N O'Connor Blvd
Ste. 2500
Irving
TX 75039-3714
USA
Tel: 972-869 3400
Fax: 972-869 6501
(Time management consulting
services)

GLOSSARY

4S this is based on four Chinese words beginning with 'S'. The English translation is Organisation, Orderliness, Neatness, Cleanliness – Eastern time management

Benchmarking comparing what you do to the best in your field

Crisis management dealing with a crisis in a way that minimises unpleasant consequences

Critical path analysis involves analysing all the steps in a complicated process, working out how the steps relate to each other and how long each takes. You can then work out in which order the steps should be done in order to complete the process in the shortest possible time (the critical path). The critical path is mapped onto a chart using overlapping lines and actual progress can be monitored by comparing it with the chart

Just-In-Time (JIT) each stage in a production process calls for parts as and when needed

Murphy's Law (or Sod's Law) if something can go wrong, it will

Pareto principle (80/20 rule) this rule was discovered by Alfredo Pareto in the nineteenth century. It states that 80 per cent of profits come from 20 per cent of the products, or 80 per cent of your results come from 20 per cent of your work. This rule can be applied to many other situations

Parkinson's Law in 1958, Cyril Northcote Parkinson stated that 'Work expands to fill the time available for its completion'

Personal Efficiency Programme (PEP) a programme designed to help an individual manage their time more effectively

Right First Time this is the name given to the aim of building quality in and ensuring that a product or piece of work is of high quality the first (and only) time it is done. Doing something in this way improves the quality and speeds up the process, thus saving time

INDEX

Other related titles

Performance Appraisals

Polly Bird

All managers have to carry out staff appraisals, and *Teach Yourself Performance Appraisals* provides the guidelines and help on how to do this effectively and obtain the desired results. The book deals with each stage of appraising, from preparation to evaluation. It also gives advice on how to cope with difficulties during the appraisal process, as well as how to handle your own appraisal.

The book is written in a practical and straightforward way and includes:

- guidance to managers new to appraisals, and those who want to improve
- advice on how to turn discussion into action
- help with upward appraisals.

Polly Bird is a professional writer of business and training books.

Other related titles

Imaginative Marketing

J Jonathan Gabay

Powerful marketing campaigns are based on original thinking and creative planning. *Teach Yourself Imaginative Marketing* concentrates on the engine which drives successful marketing – *imagination*. Revealing many profitable tips and secrets to help you target, brand and sell your enterprise whilst generating provocative publicity, this book will keep you three steps ahead of the competition.

The book:

● covers the key marketing areas of sales, advertising, PR and branding
● concentrates on the dynamic 'imaginative' side of marketing
● is easy to follow with useful activities and exercises
● includes a comprehensive 'jargon buster' section
● is suitable for anyone working in or studying marketing.

Completely up to date, ready for the cut and thrust world of marketing beyond the millennium, this book is indispensable for anyone who wants their business and careers to succeed and continue to breed success.

J Jonathan Gabay, a Course Director at the Chartered Institute of Marketing, has worked for some of the world's biggest advertising agencies and on some of the best-known marketing brands.

Other related titles

Copywriting
for Creative Advertisement

J Jonathan Gabay

You've got the greatest product or service in the world. The trouble is, no one knows about it. Now, thanks to this outstandingly informative book, whether you run a small social club, theatrical society, charity or even work for an advertising agency or international organisation, you can soon be writing powerful copy that promises to get your message across.

From planning to implementation *Teach Yourself Copywriting* explodes the mystique surrounding copywriting. In doing so it reveals all the inside secrets that will encourage people to seek out your product or service.

Step by step, Jonathan Gabay draws on his wide and extensive experience in advertising and marketing to show you in an entertaining and totally absorbing way how to turn words into the response you need. He covers every aspect of creative advertising and promotion, including:

- radio, TV, press and posters
- direct mail
- the Internet
- business-to-business
- public relations
- recruitment
- charities.

Whether you are new to copywriting or already work in an agency or marketing department, this book is indispensable. It is packed from cover to cover with all the facts you need – at your fingertips – to write powerful, compelling copy.